Terrie L. Wilson
Editor

The Twenty-First Century Art Librarian

The Twenty-First Century Art Librarian has been co-published simultaneously as *Journal of Library Administration*, Volume 39, Number 1 2003.

Pre-publication
REVIEWS,
COMMENTARIES,
EVALUATIONS . . .

"**A**N EXCELLENT COLLECTION. . . . Useful to both experienced and novice librarians. The topics covered offer a nice mix of pertinent chapters related to both academic and museum art libraries, as well as one chapter related to the very timely subject of visual resources."

Ann B. Abid
Head Librarian
Ingalls Library
The Cleveland Museum of Art

More pre-publication
REVIEWS, COMMENTARIES, EVALUATIONS . . .

" **A** N EXCELLENT OVERVIEW of issues facing library professionals in the evolving landscape of today's vibrant art library. A MUST-READ for those aspiring to be librarians, for practitioners who need reassurance and fresh insights, and most of all, for library administrators planning new initiatives. Each group will find value in time well spent between the covers of this engaging study. . . . LIVELY, HIGHLY READABLE . . . with useful facts and figures from surveys and studies gathered by leading practitioners in the field."

Christine L. Sundt, MA
Curator of Visual Resources
Architecture and Allied Arts Library
University of Chicago

The Haworth Information Press
An Imprint of The Haworth Press, Inc.

The Twenty-First Century
Art Librarian

The Twenty-First Century Art Librarian has been co-published simultaneously as *Journal of Library Administration*, Volume 39, Number 1 2003.

The *Journal of Library Administration* Monographic "Separates"·

Below is a list of "separates," which in serials librarianship means a special issue simultaneously published as a special journal issue or double-issue *and* as a "separate" hardbound monograph. (This is a format which we also call a "DocuSerial.")

"Separates" are published because specialized libraries or professionals may wish to purchase a specific thematic issue by itself in a format which can be separately cataloged and shelved, as opposed to purchasing the journal on an on-going basis. Faculty members may also more easily consider a "separate" for classroom adoption.

"Separates" are carefully classified separately with the major book jobbers so that the journal tie-in can be noted on new book order slips to avoid duplicate purchasing.

You may wish to visit Haworth's Website at . . .

http://www.HaworthPress.com

. . . to search our online catalog for complete tables of contents of these separates and related publications.

You may also call 1-800-HAWORTH (outside US/Canada: 607-722-5857), or Fax 1-800-895-0582 (outside US/Canada: 607-771-0012), or e-mail at:

docdelivery@haworthpress.com

Off-Campus Library Services, edited by Ann Marie Casey (Vol. 31, No. 3/4, 2001 and Vol. 32, No. 1/2, 2001). *This informative volume examines various aspects of off-campus, or distance learning. It explores training issues for library staff, Web site development, changing roles for librarians, the uses of conferencing software, library support for Web-based courses, library agreements and how to successfully negotiate them, and much more!*

Research Collections and Digital Information, edited by Sul H. Lee (Vol. 31, No. 2, 2000). *Offers new strategies for collecting, organizing, and accessing library materials in the digital age.*

Academic Research on the Internet: Options for Scholars & Libraries, edited by Helen Laurence, MLS, EdD, and William Miller, MLS, PhD (Vol. 30, No. 1/2/3/4, 2000). *"Emphasizes quality over quantity. . . . Presents the reader with the best research-oriented Web sites in the field. A state-of-the-art review of academic use of the Internet as well as a guide to the best Internet sites and services. . . . A useful addition for any academic library." (David A. Tyckoson, MLS, Head of Reference, California State University, Fresno)*

Management for Research Libraries Cooperation, edited by Sul H. Lee (Vol. 29. No. 3/4, 2000). *Delivers sound advice, models, and strategies for increasing sharing between institutions to maximize the amount of printed and electronic research material you can make available in your library while keeping costs under control.*

Integration in the Library Organization, edited by Christine E. Thompson, PhD (Vol. 29, No. 2, 1999). *Provides librarians with the necessary tools to help libraries balance and integrate public and technical services and to improve the capability of libraries to offer patrons quality services and large amounts of information.*

Library Training for Staff and Customers, edited by Sara Ramser Beck, MLS, MBA (Vol. 29, No. 1, 1999). *This comprehensive book is designed to assist library professionals involved in presenting or planning training for library staff members and customers. You will explore ideas for effective general reference training, training on automated systems, training in specialized subjects such as African American history and biography, and training for areas such as patents and trademarks, and business subjects.* Library Training for Staff and Customers *answers numerous training questions and is an excellent guide for planning staff development.*

Collection Development in the Electronic Environment: Shifting Priorities, edited by Sul H. Lee (Vol. 28, No. 4, 1999). *Through case studies and firsthand experiences, this volume discusses meeting the needs of scholars at universities, budgeting issues, user education, staffing in the electronic age, collaborating libraries and resources, and how vendors meet the needs of different customers.*

The Age Demographics of Academic Librarians: A Profession Apart, by Stanley J. Wilder (Vol. 28, No. 3, 1999). *The average age of librarians has been increasing dramatically since 1990. This unique book will provide insights on how this demographic issue can impact a library and what can be done to make the effects positive.*

Collection Development in a Digital Environment, edited by Sul H. Lee (Vol. 28, No. 1, 1999). *Explores ethical and technological dilemmas of collection development and gives several suggestions on how a library can successfully deal with these challenges and provide patrons with the information they need.*

Scholarship, Research Libraries, and Global Publishing, by Jutta Reed-Scott (Vol. 27, No. 3/4, 1999). *This book documents a research project in conjunction with the Association of Research Libraries (ARL) that explores the issue of foreign acquisition and how it affects collection in international studies, area studies, collection development, and practices of international research libraries.*

Managing Multicultural Diversity in the Library: Principles and Issues for Administrators, edited by Mark Winston (Vol. 27, No. 1/2, 1999). *Defines diversity, clarifies why it is important to address issues of diversity, and identifies goals related to diversity and how to go about achieving those goals.*

Information Technology Planning, edited by Lori A. Goetsch (Vol. 26, No. 3/4, 1999). *Offers innovative approaches and strategies useful in your library and provides some food for thought about information technology as we approach the millennium.*

The Economics of Information in the Networked Environment, edited by Meredith A. Butler, MLS, and Bruce R. Kingma, PhD (Vol. 26, No. 1/2, 1998). *"A book that should be read both by information professionals and by administrators, faculty and others who share a collective concern to provide the most information to the greatest number at the lowest cost in the networked environment." (Thomas J. Galvin, PhD, Professor of Information Science and Policy, University at Albany, State University of New York)*

OCLC 1967-1997: Thirty Years of Furthering Access to the World's Information, edited by K. Wayne Smith (Vol. 25, No. 2/3/4, 1998). *"A rich-and poignantly personal, at times-historical account of what is surely one of this century's most important developments in librarianship." (Deanna B. Marcum, PhD, President, Council on Library and Information Resources, Washington, DC)*

Management of Library and Archival Security: From the Outside Looking In, edited by Robert K. O'Neill, PhD (Vol. 25, No. 1, 1998). *"Provides useful advice and on-target insights for professionals caring for valuable documents and artifacts." (Menzi L. Behrnd-Klodt, JD, Attorney/Archivist, Klodt and Associates, Madison, WI)*

Economics of Digital Information: Collection, Storage, and Delivery, edited by Sul H. Lee (Vol. 24, No. 4, 1997). *Highlights key concepts and issues vital to a library's successful venture into the digital environment and helps you understand why the transition from the printed page to the digital packet has been problematic for both creators of proprietary materials and users of those materials.*

The Academic Library Director: Reflections on a Position in Transition, edited by Frank D'Andraia, MLS (Vol. 24, No. 3, 1997). *"A useful collection to have whether you are seeking a position as director or conducting a search for one." (College & Research Libraries News)*

Emerging Patterns of Collection Development in Expanding Resource Sharing, Electronic Information, and Network Environment, edited by Sul H. Lee (Vol. 24, No. 1/2, 1997). *"The issues it deals with are common to us all. We all need to make our funds go further and our resources work harder, and there are ideas here which we can all develop." (The Library Association Record)*

Interlibrary Loan/Document Delivery and Customer Satisfaction: Strategies for Redesigning Services, edited by Pat L. Weaver-Meyers, Wilbur A. Stolt, and Yem S. Fong (Vol. 23, No. 1/2, 1997). *"No interlibrary loan department supervisor at any mid-sized to large college or university library can afford not to read this book." (Gregg Sapp, MLS, MEd, Head of Access Services, University of Miami, Richter Library, Coral Gables, Florida)*

Access, Resource Sharing and Collection Development, edited by Sul H. Lee (Vol. 22, No. 4, 1996). *Features continuing investigation and discussion of important library issues, specifically the role of libraries in acquiring, storing, and disseminating information in different formats.*

Managing Change in Academic Libraries, edited by Joseph J. Branin (Vol. 22, No. 2/3, 1996). *"Touches on several aspects of academic library management, emphasizing the changes that are occurring at the present time. . . . Recommended this title for individuals or libraries interested in management aspects of academic libraries." (RQ American Library Association)*

Libraries and Student Assistants: Critical Links, edited by William K. Black, MLS (Vol. 21, No. 3/4, 1995). *"A handy reference work on many important aspects of managing student assistants. . . . Solid, useful information on basic management issues in this work and several chapters are useful for experienced managers." (The Journal of Academic Librarianship)*

The Future of Resource Sharing, edited by Shirley K. Baker and Mary E. Jackson, MLS (Vol. 21, No. 1/2, 1995). *"Recommended for library and information science schools because of its balanced presentation of the ILL/document delivery issues." (Library Acquisitions: Practice and Theory)*

The Future of Information Services, edited by Virginia Steel, MA, and C. Brigid Welch, MLS (Vol. 20, No. 3/4, 1995). *"The leadership discussions will be useful for library managers as will the discussions of how library structures and services might work in the next century." (Australian Special Libraries)*

The Dynamic Library Organizations in a Changing Environment, edited by Joan Giesecke, MLS, DPA (Vol. 20, No. 2, 1995). *"Provides a significant look at potential changes in the library world and presents its readers with possible ways to address the negative results of such changes. . . . Covers the key issues facing today's libraries . . . Two thumbs up!" (Marketing Library Resources)*

Monographic "Separates" list continued at the back

The Twenty-First Century Art Librarian

Terrie L. Wilson
Editor

The Twenty-First Century Art Librarian has been co-published simultaneously as *Journal of Library Administration*, Volume 39, Number 1 2003.

The Haworth Information Press
An Imprint of
The Haworth Press, Inc.
New York • London • Oxford

Published by

The Haworth Information Press®, 10 Alice Street, Binghamton, NY 13904-1580 USA

The Haworth Information Press® is an imprint of The Haworth Press, Inc., 10 Alice Street, Binghamton, NY 13904-1580 USA.

The Twenty-First Century Art Librarian has been co-published simultaneously as *Journal of Library Administration*, Volume 39, Number 1 2003.

The development, preparation, and publication of this work has been undertaken with great care. However, the publisher, employees, editors, and agents of The Haworth Press and all imprints of The Haworth Press, Inc., including The Haworth Medical Press® and Pharmaceutical Products Press®, are not responsible for any errors contained herein or for consequences that may ensue from use of materials or information contained in this work. Opinions expressed by the author(s) are not necessarily those of The Haworth Press, Inc. With regard to case studies, identities and circumstances of individuals discussed herein have been changed to protect confidentiality. Any resemblance to actual persons, living or dead, is entirely coincidental.

Cover design by Marylouise E. Doyle.

Library of Congress Cataloging-in-Publication Data

The twenty-first century art librarian / Terrie L. Wilson, editor.
    p. cm.
    Co-published simultaneously as Journal of library administration, v. 39, no. 1, 2003.
    Includes bibliographical references and index.
    ISBN 0-7890-2108-0 (alk. paper) – ISBN 0-7890-2109-9 (pbk. : alk. paper)
    1. Art libraries–Administration. 2. Museum libraries–Administration. 3. Libraries–Special collections. I. Wilson, Terrie L. II. Journal of library administration.
Z675.A85T88 2003
025.1'967–dc21

2003002280

Indexing, Abstracting & Website/Internet Coverage

This section provides you with a list of major indexing & abstracting services. That is to say, each service began covering this periodical during the year noted in the right column. Most Websites which are listed below have indicated that they will either post, disseminate, compile, archive, cite or alert their own Website users with research-based content from this work. (This list is as current as the copyright date of this publication.)

Abstracting, Website/Indexing Coverage......... Year When Coverage Began

- *Academic Abstracts/CD-ROM* 1993
- *Academic Search: database of 2,000 selected academic serials,*
  updated monthly: EBSCO Publishing 1995
- *Academic Search Elite (EBSCO)* 1993
- *Academic Search Premier (EBSCO)*................................... 2001
- *AGRICOLA Database <www.natl.usda.gov/ag98>* 1991
- *Business ASAP* 1993
- *CNPIEC Reference Guide: Chinese National Directory*
  of Foreign Periodicals 1995
- *Current Articles on Library Literature and Services (CALLS)*........ 1992
- *Current Cites [Digital Libraries] [Electronic Publishing] [Multimedia &*
  Hypermedia] [Networks & Networking] [General] 2000
- *Current Index to Journals in Education* 1986
- *Educational Administration Abstracts (EAA)* 1991
- *FINDEX <www.publist.com>*... 1999
- *FRANCIS. INIST/CNRS <www.inist.fr>*................................. 1986
- *General Business File ASAP <www.galegroup.com>*..................... 1993
- *General Reference Center GOLD on InfoTrac Web*...................... 1984
- *Higher Education Abstracts, providing the latest in research & theory in more*
  than 140 major topics 1991
- *IBZ International Bibliography of Periodical Literature <www.saur.de>*....... 1995
- *Index Guide to College Journals (core list compiled by integrating*
  48 indexes frequently used to support undergraduate programs
  in small to medium sized libraries) 1999

(continued)

*Special Bibliographic Notes related to special journal issues
(separates) and indexing/abstracting:*

- indexing/abstracting services in this list will also cover material in any "separate" that is co-published simultaneously with Haworth's special thematic journal issue or DocuSerial. Indexing/abstracting usually covers material at the article/chapter level.
- monographic co-editions are intended for either non-subscribers or libraries which intend to purchase a second copy for their circulating collections.
- monographic co-editions are reported to all jobbers/wholesalers/approval plans. The source journal is listed as the "series" to assist the prevention of duplicate purchasing in the same manner utilized for books-in-series.
- to facilitate user/access services all indexing/abstracting services are encouraged to utilize the co-indexing entry note indicated at the bottom of the first page of each article/chapter/contribution.
- this is intended to assist a library user of any reference tool (whether print, electronic, online, or CD-ROM) to locate the monographic version if the library has purchased this version but not a subscription to the source journal.
- individual articles/chapters in any Haworth publication are also available through the Haworth Document Delivery Service (HDDS).

The Twenty-First Century Art Librarian

CONTENTS

ABOUT THE EDITOR

Terrie L. Wilson, MLS, MA, is Art Librarian at the Michigan State University Fine Arts Library in East Lansing. She has published articles on artists' books for *Art Documentation,* the official bulletin of the Art Libraries Society of North America (ARLIS/NA), of which she is an active member. Ms. Wilson has also published numerous book reviews for *Art Documentation,* the *American Reference Books Annual,* and *Choice.*

Preface

At the beginning of the 21st century, most librarians face similar administrative issues, including inadequate staffing, the desire to keep ahead of and plan for technological change, and the need to wear multiple "hats" in terms of day-to-day responsibilities. Art librarians are no exception, but they are unique in terms of the clientele they serve, their subject knowledge, and the variety of environments in which they work. The articles in this publication highlight some of the administrative issues that are at the forefront of art librarianship today. Ideas for articles were solicited via the Art Libraries Society's listserv, ARLIS-L. Art, architecture and visual resources librarians were asked if they would address significant administrative issues of their own choosing. The resulting group of authors represents a variety of different types of art librarians including those from museum, academic, and visual resources libraries. Not represented are librarians from large museum or art and design school libraries; these categories of art librarianship are significant, and it is my hope that future publications will address the challenges faced by librarians in these areas.

This publication is not intended to serve as a new primer on art librarianship. Rather, the articles included offer a glimpse into the world of art library administration at the beginning of the 21st century. The volume is divided into three parts, focusing on the individuals who work in art libraries, the collections they maintain, and a comparison of common practices in the field. Two articles comprise the first part; one addresses staffing standards at all levels in an academic art or architecture library. Professional, paraprofessional, and student staff are discussed in terms of training and performance expectations. The other article describes the working environment of the small art museum library; generally op-

[Haworth co-indexing entry note]: "Preface." Wilson, Terrie L. Co-published simultaneously in *Journal of Library Administration* (The Haworth Information Press, an imprint of The Haworth Press, Inc.) Vol. 39, No. 1, 2003, pp. xv-xvi; and: *The Twenty-First Century Art Librarian* (ed: Terrie L. Wilson) The Haworth Information Press, an imprint of The Haworth Press, Inc., 2003, pp. xiii-xiv. Single or multiple copies of this article are available for a fee from The Haworth Document Delivery Service [1-800-HAWORTH, 9:00 a.m. - 5:00 p.m. (EST). E-mail address: docdelivery@haworthpress.com].

erated by solo professionals, the small art museum librarian experiences challenges and rewards unlike those in other areas of the profession.

The second section offers insight on topics from two different ends of the spectrum. From the world more commonly known as "slide librarianship" comes a discussion on the integration of digitization into the everyday operation of a visual resources library. As technology changes the way "book" librarians do their jobs, "image" librarians are experiencing similar upheaval. The article addresses how digitization is changing the very nature of these libraries and offers practical advice on how to cope with these changes. The next article discusses the servicing of special collections within a departmental or branch architecture library. Although written from the point of view of an architecture librarian, many of the issues discussed are applicable to any art library that houses a special collection. Caring for and providing access to our more unique holdings can be difficult, but the wealth of scholarly potential contained in these materials makes the challenge worthwhile.

The final section contains two articles that provide an overview of practices in different types of art libraries. A comparison between the academic art library and its museum counterpart demonstrates how institutional culture and mission affect each uniquely, as due the needs of a varied clientele. The next article, and last in the volume, presents the results of an exhaustive survey of over 150 art libraries in North America. The survey results are concentrated on four areas: instruction, facilities, digital image collections, and the impact of the Internet on acquisitions. The data provided by the survey is invaluable and will likely inspire others in the profession to evaluate their own practices.

I would anticipate that the wealth of knowledge and experience brought forward by the authors in this publication would be invaluable to other art, architecture, and visual resources librarians. It is my hope that the articles in this volume will provide non-art librarians the chance to understand some of the issues faced by art library administrators.

I would like to thank Sul Lee, editor of the *Journal of Library Administration,* for his assistance throughout the preparation of this collection. I would also like to thank the group of talented and hard-working librarians who found the time to contribute articles to this publication.

Terrie L. Wilson

Staffing Standards and Core Competencies in Academic Art and Architecture Departmental Libraries: A Preliminary Study

Sarah E. McCleskey

SUMMARY. The nature of academic departmental libraries frequently requires that professional, paraprofessional and student staff perform a variety of overlapping job functions. Literature is reviewed regarding staffing standards in academic departmental libraries and the blurring of responsibilities between professional and paraprofessional staff. The author presents results from a survey of heads of academic art and architec-

Sarah E. McCleskey is Branch Head, Gunnin Architectural Library, 112 Lee Hall, Clemson University, Clemson, SC 29634-0501. She is a member of the Art Libraries Society of North America.

[Haworth co-indexing entry note]: "Staffing Standards and Core Competencies in Academic Art and Architecture Departmental Libraries: A Preliminary Study." McCleskey, Sarah E. Co-published simultaneously in *Journal of Library Administration* (The Haworth Information Press, an imprint of The Haworth Press, Inc.) Vol. 39, No. 1, 2003, pp. 1-21; and: *The Twenty-First Century Art Librarian* (ed: Terrie L. Wilson) The Haworth Information Press, an imprint of The Haworth Press, Inc., 2003, pp. 1-21. Single or multiple copies of this article are available for a fee from The Haworth Document Delivery Service [1-800-HAWORTH, 9:00 a.m. - 5:00 p.m. (EST). E-mail address: docdelivery@haworthpress.com].

10.1300/J111v39n01_01

ture libraries. The survey focused on differing levels of staff in art and architecture libraries, types of training received, and core competencies in library skills and resources for employees at the various levels. The survey was not intended to produce conclusive results, but rather to gain information, explore trends, offer observations, and provide clarification of topics that could be considered in further research. *[Article copies available for a fee from The Haworth Document Delivery Service: 1-800-HAWORTH. E-mail address: <docdelivery@haworthpress.com> Website: <http://www.HaworthPress.com>*

KEYWORDS. Academic art library, acquisitions, access, accreditation, AMICO, architecture, architecture libraries, ARLIS, artists, ARL, branch library, cataloging, circulation, competencies, databases, departmental libraries, instruction, paraprofessional, professional staff, public services, reference, reserves, skills, solo librarian, staffing standards, student staff, support staff, survey, training, visual resources

Does your library have enough staff? Just enough? It's doubtful many would answer that they are overstaffed. Do you have the right type of staff members to carry out your mission? The nature of academic departmental libraries frequently requires that professional, paraprofessional and student staff perform a variety of overlapping job functions. Often there is only one "professional" librarian, and job responsibilities can become blurred between work performed by professional librarians, visual resources professionals, paraprofessional or clerical staff, and student employees. After reviewing the literature regarding staffing standards in academic departmental libraries and the blurring of responsibilities between "professional" and "paraprofessional" staff,[1] the author will present results from a survey of heads of academic art and architecture libraries. The survey focused on differing levels of staff in art and architecture libraries, types of training received, and core competencies in library skills and resources for employees at the various levels. The survey was not intended to produce conclusive results, but rather to gain information, explore trends, offer observations, and provide clarification of topics to be considered for future study. For purposes of the survey, academic departmental libraries were defined as those affiliated with main library systems but housed in remote locations or working as a separate entity within a main library; it did not include collections integrated with main library holdings.

A literature review must cover a dual range of topics for the present subject. The first is the area of staffing standards in academic branch libraries. There have been several studies in this area, the most significant for this topic performed by the Art Libraries Society of North America (ARLIS/NA). A second area concerns staffing competencies and job responsibilities. Literature in this area is geared to libraries as a whole with the exception of proceedings from an ARLIS/NA conference session on staff training issues. There are different opinions and data for levels of staff and their abilities to take on certain responsibilities, and the present study will address not what the various levels of staff *should* be doing, but in fact what they *are* doing.

STAFFING STANDARDS

Library literature has been somewhat sparse in its treatment of staffing issues in academic branch libraries. Robert A. Seal's 1986 chapter "Academic Branch Libraries" in *Advances in Librarianship* confirms what this author found in attempting to research staffing issues in branch libraries: "Services, collections, staffing, faculty involvement, and other concerns have all been considered in the literature, though not with the frequency nor the intensity of the centralization debate."[2] A section on staffing includes numbers and levels, although there are generally too many variables for a specific formula to be used to determine adequate numbers of professionals and paraprofessionals.[3] Seal also discusses personnel management, attributes the departmental librarian should possess, problems of staff coverage, and relations with local faculty and the main library.[4]

In 1984-85, Carolyn A. Snyder and Stella Bentley of Indiana University Libraries, Bloomington, Indiana, conducted a study to examine staff utilization in four branch libraries (Fine Arts, Biology, Journalism, and Library and Information Science).[5] The purpose of the study was to compare public services staff's perceptions of the utilization of their time with the actual recorded use. Responsibilities were divided between public services, technical services, collection development, and administration; estimates were provided for time spent on these activities by professional staff, support staff, and student assistants. To determine actual time utilization, staff recorded activities for fifteen minute segments of time on a form devised by the conductors of the survey and by personnel in the branch libraries. Each library showed a much higher percentage of time spent on public service than on the other activities.

An interesting figure shows that while branch heads estimated an average of over 33% of time spent on public service, in reality the time ranged from 4.9% (Fine Arts) to 17.2% (Journalism) with an average of 8.4%. Branch heads spent most of their time in administrative activities; this finding may be relevant for the present study, especially for libraries with a solo professional attempting to be an administrator and a reference librarian simultaneously. Conversely, branch heads estimated that they spent 30% on administrative activities when in reality they spent 70.8% on average.

The study showed that since branch heads spent most of their time on admistration, support staff and students held primary responsibility for public services. Biology and Fine Arts (the larger branches) employed support staff for public services as well as technical services, and their time estimates were accurate for public services but not for technical services and administrative activities. Supervisory support staff spent a greater amount of time on administration than estimated; generally this time was spent on supervision and planning.

The study also examined the role of student hourly employees. Most of their time was spent on public service, especially circulation, shelving, and reserves. The smaller libraries, Journalism and Library and Information Science, used students for a broader range of activities.

The summary for this study is relevant to the topic at hand and should be allowed to speak for itself:

> This study shows that there is a need to examine further and assess the functions being performed by various staffing levels within branch library units. It is important to determine what functions are appropriate to each staffing level, and to insure that proper training is provided for all employees. The key public service role of student employees requires that they must be trained and prepared for such work. Support staff must be given adequate training to develop the necessary skills for the variety of tasks and responsibilities needed in a public services unit. Finally this study strongly indicates the necessity for librarians to have administrative abilities. Clearly, both preservice and inservice education must provide the background and skills required for individuals who are so heavily involved in administrative functions.[6]

In 1995, the Staffing Standards Committee of the Art Libraries Society of North America completed a study begun in 1988, a revision of an earlier study of staffing standards for Art Libraries and Visual Resources Collections.[7] The standards were designed to assist art libraries and visual resources collections in determining staffing needs. This thorough study embraced the need for self-study, examining institutional goals, and reviewing the mission of the specialized collection within the institutional context. Additionally, tools for establishing local criteria for self-assessment were suggested.

The standards stress the need to set staffing goals and objectives within the context of the parent institution. By assessing the current environment and resources, art libraries and visual resources collections can determine priorities for the collection and strategies for achieving them. The process of setting goals should involve representatives from all relevant constituencies; communication is vital to the success of such a project. Self-assessment and strategic planning should produce guidelines for the library or collection to outline its staffing needs in a manner consistent with institutional and local goals. These documents might be used to justify requests for increased staffing, retention, or reorganization of current staffing levels.[8] The study provides an appendix that can guide libraries or visual resources collections in self-assessment and goal development.[9]

Staffing standards for professionals, paraprofessionals and technical staff, and other support staff are outlined. Professionals are expected to have graduate-level education, knowledge of library and information management, and specialized knowledge in the field of art; these requirements would vary based on the responsibilities of a particular position. Examples of professional-type responsibilities are outlined in Appendix B (goal setting, personnel management, collection management, budget administration, reference services, cataloging and classification, systems management, circulation, public relations, participation in the institutional community and in the professional community).[10] Paraprofessionals and technical staff are defined as higher-level support personnel. They normally would be supervised by professionals. Their job duties require special knowledge, skills, abilities or education as well as decision-making abilities. Examples of responsibilities include reference and patron assistance, access services, cataloging or processing, collection development, supervision of clerical staff, collection maintenance, and daily operations.[11] Other support staff generally perform process-oriented tasks not requiring higher education or special skills. These tasks might include daily operations, circulation, acquisitions, processing, and supervision of students. Student workers can be expected to perform process-oriented tasks as well.[12]

The main goal of art or architecture libraries in academic systems is to support the mission of the institution and the curriculum of programs served (for example, studio art, architecture, history of art, etc.). Collections and services must comply with accreditation standards. The ARLIS/NA standards discuss differing scenarios for collections in academic institutions and state that as a minimum requirement, these collections need professional level subject specialists to work on collection development, public service, and library instruction, and to serve as faculty liaisons. Ideally they should hold faculty or tenure-track positions.[13]

A recent Association of Research Libraries (ARL) SPEC Kit, "Branch Libraries and Discrete Collections," examines several aspects of branch libraries through a survey of 54 ARL libraries.[14] The survey examines evolving circumstances and technologies to determine why organizations decide to close, add, or merge branch library collections. Staffing is only a small part of the survey but an interesting finding relates to percentages of FTE staff in branch libraries. Of the 54 libraries surveyed, 26% of staff were professional librarians, 43% were support staff, 22% were student assistants, 5% were clerical staff, and 4% were other professionals. This distribution mirrored distribution of employees among total library staff; 88% of branch libraries had a professional librarian working on site.[15]

DIVISION OF RESPONSIBILITIES: VARYING VIEWPOINTS

A hot topic in librarianship is the blurring of responsibilities between professional librarians (MLS holders) and paraprofessionals (non-MLS library staff). For example, paraprofessionals may work at reference desks, perform original cataloging, or serve in capacities such as head of serials acquisitions. This discussion can cause heated debate and often some rancor between the two groups. In branch libraries, where most employees must know how to perform most tasks, the lines are even more blurred. Much has been written, and no doubt will continue to be written, on the topic. The reference desk has been a particular point of debate. It is an appropriate subject for this study as branch libraries frequently rely on main libraries for such services as cataloging and serials processing, whereas reference service must be provided onsite. A brief survey here will present a study with unfavorable results regarding paraprofessionals working at the reference desk, some arguments and factors affecting success in this situation, and some practical examples from an Ask ARLIS session on training paraprofessionals and other support staff for performing quality reference work. In Ask

ARLIS sessions (held at ARLIS/NA annual conferences) three to four panelists discuss a variety of ideas and perspectives on the given topic.

In 1988 Marjorie Murfin and Charles Bunge published results of a study that was part of the Wisconsin-Ohio Reference Evaluation Program.[16] The study utilized a computer-readable form to gather information from patrons and library staff regarding reference transactions. Thirty-three academic libraries volunteered to participate in the study; it was therefore not random but did represent libraries of all sizes. The computerized form (Reference Transaction Assessment Instrument, or RTAI) allowed libraries to gather data on the success of answers to reference questions from both patron and library staff points of view.

Success was achieved when a patron marked that s/he got just what was wanted, was fully satisfied, and did not mark any of the reasons for being less than satisfied. Paraprofessionals were found to have performed at a significantly lower level than professional librarians. The case was similar with the "fully satisfied" question.[17] Patrons were queried regarding perceptions of quality of service received, and in this paraprofessionals received lower ratings except in regard to courtesy.[18] The study also supported the argument that the paraprofessional may have more difficulty communicating with patrons and negotiating reference questions; more often patrons felt that paraprofessionals had not understood their questions. As stated by the authors, "[L]ibrarian awareness of communication difficulty was significantly less common among paraprofessionals than it was among professionals."[19] In working with specific question and patron types, paraprofessionals were found to be significantly less successful when performing a subject search in the library catalog, and when answering questions for freshmen and sophomores (the authors assumed questions from underclass students would be less complex and therefore easier to answer). Additionally, paraprofessionals scored lower on questions with higher degrees of complexity, and spent shorter time periods working on questions.[20] Finally, the survey compared success of paraprofessionals when working in consultation with professionals on answering reference questions, and found that in consultation patrons' satisfaction was significantly higher.[21]

While the information from this study may be somewhat daunting, the authors looked more specifically at relationships between paraprofessionals and professional librarians in specific libraries, and found that when the two worked in consultation they achieved significant effectiveness. Paraprofessionals in these libraries also worked more closely with patrons rather than just directing them to possible sources of information.[22] It is interesting that the level of training paraprofessionals received was not factored into the study. The authors of the study conclude:

> It is clear that academic libraries that use paraprofessional staff at the reference desk cannot routinely assume that such use is effective. Instead, such libraries should carefully assess the effectiveness with which reference questions are answered, using their patrons' perceptions and other relevant data. Such assessment, along with careful study of libraries where paraprofessional staff members are performing effectively, can be the basis for optimum staffing patterns for this important library service.

In her recent monograph *The Library Paraprofessional: Notes from the Underground*, Terry Rodgers gives an interesting historical account of non-MLS library staff; one chapter in particular focuses on the issue of paraprofessionals at the reference desk.[23] She reports that despite studies such as the one conducted by Murfin and Bunge, 88% of Association of Research Libraries (ARL) and 66% of smaller college and university libraries regularly employee paraprofessionals at the reference desk.[24] In the past, before an ALA-accredited MLS became a requirement for a "professional" position, most librarians' training was on-the-job rather than formal. Rodgers reports that many graduate MLS programs increasingly recognize that on-the-job training is as valuable, if not more, than formal classroom education; she feels that MLS librarians who started their careers as paraprofessionals are much better prepared for the real working environment.[25] This author, through personal experience, agrees. If a person possesses what might be called the "reference gene," then MLS or no MLS, he or she will be able to provide quality services. Rodgers emphasizes the importance of adequate training to prepare any employee to work in reference.[26]

Rodgers cites a number of studies from the 1980s (including the study by Murfin and Bunge) that present negative views of paraprofessionals working at the reference desk. Some of the quotes from these studies might be interpreted as invective against paraprofessional employees. For example, Nancy Emmick's study of academic library reference practices refers to "nonprofessional" employees as overzealous in attempting to help patrons; she states that these employees would best serve to recognize the types of questions that should be answered by a professional librarian.[27] (Anecdotally, one librarian who responded to the present survey made a similar comment.) To be fair, Emmick includes a statement that using nonprofessionals at the reference desk is "neither all good nor all bad,"[28] but Rodgers does not take kindly to her characterizations of non-MLS employees: "She [Emmick] sees nonprofessionals at the reference desk as useful low-cost creatures, albeit a mite too enthusiastic, like large, immature dogs apt to prance up to people and place muddy paws on shoulders . . ."[29] Emmick states that it should be clear to patrons which employees are nonprofessionals and which are MLS librarians, perhaps by "badges, signs, physical separation, and any other useful means."[30] Rodgers responds that "whips, fetters, or pens" might also be appropriate.[31] Emmick further suggests (on a positive note?) that nonprofessionals may improve the morale of professional reference librarians by relieving some of their anxiety at peak periods of reference activity.[32]

Rodgers points to several studies that examine the competency of professional librarians at answering reference questions, where correct answers averaged around 55 or 60%.[33] Throughout the chapter on paraprofessionals at the reference desk, she mentions the lack of adequate training provided for various levels of staff including professional librarians, paraprofessionals and student staff.[34] A lack of adequate training is offered as the most reasonable explanation for differences in performance between professional librarians, paraprofessionals, and student employees: "Lack of on-the-job training and experience are the greatest and most inexplicable lacunae in the whole phenomenon of nonprofessional reference-desk performance."[35] She singles out the study by Murfin and Bunge as incomplete as no provision was made for educational background, length of employment, or formal training programs for the paraprofessionals who scored so much lower than the professional librarians.[36] Rodgers sums up the chapter by stating that when paraprofessionals are relied upon to work the reference desk, libraries must implement comprehensive training programs to advance staff development not only for non-MLS employees but for all library staff.[37]

For a look at paraprofessionals and support staff working in art libraries, it is helpful to turn to proceedings from the 20th annual ARLIS/NA Conference held in Chicago in 1992. Patricia Lynagh of the Smithsonian American Art Museum moderated a session sponsored by the Reference Section titled "Training Paraprofessionals and Support Staff for Reference Work in the Art Library."[38] Using the term paraprofessionals to define volunteers, student employees, and staff without an MLS, panelists discussed the types of tasks assigned to paraprofessionals, expectations for answering inquiries, formal training programs, and the use of student workers in the functioning of the academic art library.

Laurie Whitehill (now Laurie Whitehill Chong) of the Rhode Island School of Design, discussed the pros and cons of hiring student employees to handle reference queries at her institution. As in many departmental libraries, professional librarians were present during the day but replaced by students during evening hours. Students were hired based on past work experience (particularly in libraries) and responsibilities, and positive communication skills. Training was conducted individually and in groups, including library orientation and demonstration of important reference sources. A manual was maintained to assist students in answering questions. At the time, students' success in answering questions was not monitored, but this was something that would be desirable for the future. Some negative aspects of using student employees for nights and weekends were lack of supervision, inaccurate answering of queries, and possible discouragement for patrons. Turnover rate among student employees was high, making training time all the more time consuming. Successful students were rewarded by promotion. In general, Chong felt that students provided adequate limited service but that more difficult questions should be handled by professional librarians.[39]

Barbara Reed, then Art Librarian at Dartmouth College's Sherman Art Library, spoke about training procedures she developed for student assistants, including reference interviewing, online catalog, and philosophy of reference. Students at the Sherman library worked the reference desk from 9 p.m. until midnight throughout the week and on weekends. When hiring students, Reed found a college degree and positive communication skills with patrons desirable. Training was progressive, moving from circulation skills and serials check-in to reference responsibilities. Training was ongoing and geared to the individual's background. Reed included how to find information on artists' biographies as well as how to use appropriate indexes, abstracts, and other important bibliographic tools. Directional questions were also covered; a "cheat sheet" with answers to often-asked directional questions was kept at the reference desk. Students were instructed to refer in-depth queries to professional librarians, filling out a written request for assistance when there was no librarian on duty. Future plans included a task force to discuss staff training for reference and an audiotape to facilitate more hands-on training.[40]

Margaret Myers of the American Library Association (ALA) office for Library Personnel Resources spoke about initiatives for training support staff in public libraries, dealing with certification, compensation, terminology, and role definition. These could all translate into the academic library environment. She described a study showing that in larger libraries, paraprofessionals often work at the professional level, doing reference work, collection development, and online database searching. In a positive light, she stressed that paraprofessionals bring a variety of backgrounds and education to their jobs. Surveys found that paraprofessionals want more opportunities for job-specific training. Continuing education programs, conferences, and workshops can provide development of skills and opportunities for career advancement.[41]

The third panelist was Mary Goulding, director of reference service at the Suburban Library System in Oak Lawn, Illinois. She held responsibilities for training in 235 public, academic, and educational libraries. These libraries had compulsory reference standards, including standards for training. All staff members working the reference desk were required to take a workshop in conducting reference interviews; staff without an MLS were required to take five workshops. Goulding felt that implementation of the standards was successful. She discussed some particular training methods to ensure success for paraprofessionals at the reference desk, including question-centered training, listening skills, and having detailed instructions for handling questions. Karen L. Meizner, an RLIN search trainer, also spoke about the importance of thorough training for paraprofessionals.[42]

During the discussion session, a question was raised about how a librarian might feel when a paraprofessional was performing the same or similar duties; the response was that with good teamwork and cross-training, the morale of both employees could be raised. Myers added that changing of role and role definitions can contribute to mutual respect between the two types of employees.[43]

Having examined some issues in staffing standards and overlapping duties in departmental libraries, we turn to a survey conducted to collect data regarding responsibilities of different types of employees in academic art and architecture libraries. This survey is intended to yield information about differences between duties staff are formally assigned, and actual expectations for knowledge, skills and abilities. It will also provide information about the overlap in job responsibilities that has been discussed above.

ACADEMIC ART AND ARCHITECTURE BRANCH LIBRARIES SURVEY

The survey was conducted over the World Wide Web in May 2002. Recipients targeted as heads of academic art and architecture branch libraries were invited to participate by email. A general email with the URL for the survey was also sent to the ARLIS/NA listserv to notify library heads that may not have been contacted. The list of recipients was generated from the ARLIS/NA membership directory and from the membership of the Association of Architecture School Librarians. The survey was sent to 116 targeted recipients. Thirty-three responses were received. Of these, two were "outliers," a term used to denote surveys that were incomplete or unacceptable because of radically inconsistent data. Consequently 31 surveys were valid, a 27 percent response rate. Unfortunately, the response rate is not high enough to give the survey statistical validity, but it does provide anecdotal evidence for a range of academic art and architecture branch libraries in the U.S. and Canada. Appendices A and B provide information on size of respondents' library collections and number of staff employed in these facilities.

The survey addressed which type of staff perform various duties, what types of training are provided for these responsibilities at the different levels of staffing, and what are considered to be core competencies for the various staff levels. Participants were provided opportunity to make comments. Table 1 outlines the different staff levels represented among the 30 libraries; this does not represent the number of each type of staff within a particular library. For the purposes of this survey, staff were divided into six categories: students, lower level support staff (performing process-oriented tasks), paraprofessionals or technical staff members (staff who do not have MLS or equivalent but whose job duties require special skills and/or education), visual resources professionals (staff with MFA, BFA, extensive visual resources experience and/or training), MLS or equivalent librarians, and "other" staff. Participants were asked to provide additional information when the category "other" was used. Table 1 also provides percentages of libraries employing various staff types.

Table 1 demonstrates that most academic art and architecture libraries employ student workers, and approximately half employ lower level

TABLE 1. Number of Libraries with Various Staffing Levels

Staff Type	Students	Lower Level Support Staff	Paraprofessional or Technical Staff	Visual Resources Professionals	MLS Librarians	Other
Number of Libraries	29	16	25	8	31	3
Percentage of Libraries	93.5%	51.6%	80.6%	25.8%	100%	9.6%

support staff. It is encouraging that many libraries are able to employ higher level paraprofessional or technical staff. The percentage of visual resources professionals is low, but this is to be expected as many visual resources collections are maintained by academic departmental staff rather than libraries. Every participating library employs an MLS librarian; a few of the respondents, however, reported that the MLS librarian was not a full time employee.

One of the purposes of the survey was to investigate how different libraries assign responsibilities for common tasks to their employees. These tasks included circulation, interlibrary loan, reserves, visual resources or work with non-print media, copier or printing tasks, equipment maintenance, directional questions, reference services, bibliographic instruction, cataloging and classification, and systems management. Table 2.1 provides raw results of this query; Table 2.2 provides percentages of staff performing tasks in relation to the percentage of libraries employing the various types of staff (for example, if 16 libraries employ lower level support staff, and 8 libraries responded that lower level support staff are responsible for interlibrary loan, then the percentage would be 53.3).

Table 2.1 shows that most library staff are expected to perform circulation responsibilities. Many respondents commented that certain functions are supported by the main library; most often these were copying and printing, equipment maintenance, cataloging and classification, and systems management (the "*"'s are used to represent responses

TABLE 2.1. Staff Responsible for Common Library Tasks (Raw Data)

Responsible Staff	Students	Lower Level Support Staff	Paraprofessional or Technical Staff	Visual Resources Professionals	MLS Librarians	Other	Not Applicable
Tasks:							
Circulation	29	15	22	4	21	1	0
Interlibrary Loan	4	8	12	0	10	2	0
Reserves	8	8	22	2	11	0	2
Visual Resources	6	3	7	8	7	0	20
Copier/Printing	13	9	13	1	8	6	7
Equipment Maintenance	8	8	18	1	9	7	5
Directional Questions	29	16	21	5	25	1	0
Reference	10	11	21	5	29	1	0
Bibliographic Instruction	2	6	2	3	31	0	0
Cataloging/Classification	2	6	1	1	11	9	9
Systems Management	0	0	3	2	3	10	8

TABLE 2.2. Percentages of Staff Responsible for Common Library Tasks (Based on Number of Libraries Employing Various Types of Staff)

Responsible Staff	Students	Lower Level Support Staff	Paraprofessional or Technical Staff	Visual Resources Professionals	MLS Librarians	Other
Tasks:						
Circulation	100%	93.7%	88%	50%	67.7%	33.3%
Interlibrary Loan	13.7%	50%	48%	0%	32.2%	0%
Reserves	27.5%	50%	88%	25%	35.4%	0%
Visual Resources	20.6%	18.7%	28%	100%	22.5%	0%
Copier/Printing	44.8%	56.2%	52%	12.5%	25.8%	*
Equipment Maintenance	27.5%	50%	72%	12.5%	29%	*
Directional Questions	100%	100%	84%	62.55%	80.6%	33.3%
Reference	34.4%	68.7%	84%	62.5%	93.5%	33.3%
Bibliographic Instruction	6.8%	37.5%	8%	37.5%	100%	0%
Cataloging/Classification	6.8%	37.5%	4%	12.5%	35.4%	*
Systems Management	0%	0%	12%	25%	9.6%	*

when "other" indicated external employees, not those employed by the branch library). Most employees were expected to answer directional questions. Reference services were more likely to be performed by higher level employees such as paraprofessional/technical staff or MLS librarians. One respondent commented that during evening hours, when there is no librarian on duty, students often answer simple reference questions, thus only students with a background in art are hired.

The next part of the survey dealt with the types of training various employee categories receive for the tasks outlined above. While the survey requested responses for each category of employee, Table 3 presents the results in a compilation of the categories. Training types listed in the survey included formal (local or off-site classroom training), hands-on, one-on-one, on-the-job, and other. If respondents marked "other" they were asked to explain what was meant. The compilation of all staff types with all training types is not ideal; however, the author realized that for the training type information to be valid, one would need to tie it closely to the question of responsibilities for each type of staff member. For example, several libraries reported that students were trained in bibliographic instruction and reference services, while only a small number reported that students actually held those responsibilities. There are similar examples throughout the responses; this could be corrected in a future study.

Despite the compilation and its drawbacks, trends can be recognized from the data. The fact that libraries reported that staff are trained in ar-

TABLE 3. Training Types

Training Type	Formal	Hands-On	One-on-One	On-the-Job	Other	Not Applicable
Tasks:						
Circulation	20	82	93	102	6	38
Interlibrary Loan	4	35	36	45	0	106
Reserves	10	60	57	75	5	79
Visual Resources	6	25	35	39	0	109
Copier/Printing	1	39	41	55	4	96
Equipment Maintenance	6	44	48	60	3	93
Directional Questions	9	64	81	103	2	49
Reference	22	54	65	80	7	67
Bibliographic Instruction	15	35	34	48	5	95
Cataloging/Classification	9	22	26	29	2	122
Systems Management	20	18	22	27	2	125

eas outside their scope of responsibility points to the hypothesis that in branch libraries staff often cover a variety of areas that may lie outside their formal job description. Another interesting trend is that in all categories (excluding "other" or "not applicable") except systems management, formal training was by far the least-often type employed. One respondent found the questions on reference, bibliographic instruction and directional questions "troubling" as the only training the respondent had received for these sorts of things was in library school. On-the-job was the highest in every category where applicable; the differences between formal training and on-the-job training in directional questions, reference, and bibliographic instruction seems particularly interesting. This suggests topics for further inquiry: Is formal training available? Does the administration support formal training programs with scheduling flexibility and funding? What are the differences between opportunities for MLS librarians and other staff types? What types of training are the most effective? These issues and more could be addressed in a future study.

The final part of the survey addressed core competencies for various levels of staff. The author devised a list of knowledge, skills and abilities from personal experience and from some of the literature cited, particularly the publications from *Art Documentation*. These included customer service skills, directional questions, online catalog searching, circulation procedures, reference interviewing, philosophy of reference, information on artists' or architects' biography, use of Art Index, Avery Index, and other electronic databases, web searching, knowledge of print reference sources, locating visual resources, and equipment maintenance. There are other skills that could be addressed in future studies. Table 4.1 provides raw data for each skill considered a core competency in relation to each staffing level. Table 4.2 provides percentages of staff expected to have competency in the area in question in relation to the percentage of libraries employing the various types of staff (for example, if 16 libraries employ lower level support staff, and 12 libraries responded that lower level support staff should possess customer service skills, then the percentage would be 75). Items with a "*" in Table 4.2 show where competencies indicated were higher than the number of staff employed in responding libraries.

Percentages in Table 4.2 reveal some of the overlap between paraprofessional staff and MLS librarians discussed in the literature. For example, 76% of paraprofessionals are expected to have reference interviewing skills. The percentage of lower-level support staff expected to be able to conduct reference interviews (56%) is surprising. Higher-level staff are expected to have more familiarity with reference tools, but the percentage for paraprofessionals is also fairly high. Most staff are expected to have circulation skills and be able to answer direc-

TABLE 4.1. Core Competencies for Various Staff Types (Raw Data)

Staff type	Students	Lower Level Support Staff	Paraprofessional or Technical Staff	Visual Resources Professionals	MLS Librarians	Other	Not Applicable
Knowledge, Skills and Abilities							
Customer Service Skills	30	10	12	8	30	0	0
Directional Questions	29	20	23	7	30	0	
Online Catalog	24	19	24	8	30	0	1
Circulation Procedures	28	19	21	7	22	1	0
Reference Interviewing	3	9	19	5	30	1	0
Philosophy of Reference	1	2	17	5	30	0	1
Artist/Architect Biography	5	8	17	5	30	1	0
Art Index	10	6	19	5	30	0	0
Avery Index	7	9	15	4	28	0	0
Other Electronic Databases	8	5	19	5	29	0	1
Web Searching	7	8	21	5	31	0	0
Print Reference Sources	4	5	20	4	28	0	0
Locating Visual Resources	2	5	13	7	26	0	1
Equipment Maintenance	9	9	15	2	12	4	10

TABLE 4.2. Core Competencies for Various Staff Types (Based on Number of Libraries Employing Various Types of Staff)

Staff type	Students	Lower Level Support Staff	Paraprofessional or Technical Staff	Visual Resources Professionals	MLS Librarians	Other
Knowledge, Skills and Abilities						
Customer Service Skills	96.7%	62.5%	48%	100%	96.7%	0%
Directional Questions	93.5%	125%*	92%	87.5%	96.7%	0%
Online Catalog	77.4%	118.7%*	96%	100%	96.7%	0%
Circulation Procedures	90.3%	118.7%*	84%	87.5%	70.9%	33.3%
Reference Interviewing	9.6%	56.2%	76%	62.5%	96.7%	33.3%
Philosophy of Reference	3.2%	12.5%	68%	62.5%	96.7%	0%
Artist/Architect Biography	16.1%	50%	68%	62.5%	96.7%	33.3%
Art Index	32.2%	37.5%	76%	62.5%	96.7%	0%
Avery Index	22.5%	56.2%	60%	50%	90.3%	0%
Other Electronic Databases	25.8%	31.2%	76%	62.5%	93.5%	0%
Web Searching		50%	84%	62.5%	100%	0%
Print Reference Sources	22.5%	31.2%	80%	50%	90.3%	0%
Locating Visual Resources	6.4%	31.2%	52%	87.5%	83.8%	0%
Equipment Maintenance	29%	56.2%	60%	25%	38.7%	133.3%*

tional questions. A future study would examine statistical significance of differences in the percentages above.

Respondents had many interesting comments about this section. There were suggestions for additional categories, and these would go hand-in-hand with training issues. In particular, there were suggestions for competencies in emergency procedures, collection development, budgeting, and administrative skills. Participants were asked to identify other electronic databases employees were required to use. These included Bibliography of the History of Art, Grove Art Online, ArtBibliographies Modern, DYABOLA, Perseus, Thesaurus Linguae Graecae, WorldCat, RLIN, AMICO, and a host of multidisciplinary databases. One respondent noted that their library system subscribes to around 200 electronic databases, of which approximately one-third are relevant to art or architecture topics.

A final question asked if respondents were satisfied with the skill level of the staff in their library, and what they would like to change about the way their library is staffed. Several respondents indicated the difficulty of relying heavily on student employees; many would like to add more paraprofessional staff or professional librarians to ease the reliance on students. Some felt very satisfied that their staff were highly skilled at their job. One respondent commented that within a state library system, it is difficult to get rid of full-time employees who are not pulling their own weight, despite additional training. More comments in this section of the survey would have been useful, and this would be something to elaborate upon in a future survey.

Overall, the impression the survey gives is that in art and architecture branch libraries, many different types of staff must carry out many different responsibilities, and that different types of training are employed for these tasks. Each branch library has its own unique situation, and this makes it difficult to evaluate skills such as cataloging, copying, interlibrary loan, equipment maintenance and systems management; there are many different individuals responsible for these tasks, with responsibilities varying from library system to library system. The overlap created in branch libraries because of the relatively small number of staff indicates that it is important that staff be flexible and willing to take on responsibilities that might not fall under their formal job description. As one respondent put it, "We all pitch in and help when service is needed, though it might be the responsibility of another staff member." With this attitude, branch libraries will provide a higher level of service to patrons despite difficulties of staffing, training, and of course budgets. A more formal future survey should further examine staff overlap issues and how they can be used to improve service in art and architecture branch libraries.

NOTES

1. "Paraprofessional" is used as a term of convenience to encompass titles such as Library Assistant, Library Associate, Library Technical Assistant, and other terms used to describe non-MLS library staff members.

2. Robert A. Seal, "Academic Branch Libraries," in *Advances in Librarianship* 14 (1986) 175-209.

3. Ibid., 189.

4. Ibid., 189-192.

5. Carolyn A. Snyder and Stella Bentley, "Staff Utilization in Branch Libraries: A Research Report," in *Energies for Transition: Proceedings of the Fourth National Conference of the Association of College and Research Libraries, Baltimore, Maryland, April 9-12, 1986*, 146-151. Chicago: Association of College and Research Libraries, 1986.

6. Ibid., 148.

7. "Staffing Standards for Art Libraries and Visual Resources Collections," *Art Documentation* (Winter 1995) 27-32.

8. Ibid., 28-28.

9. Ibid., 30-31.

10. Ibid., 31.

11. Ibid.

12. Ibid., 29.

13. Ibid., 28.

14. Karen S. Croneis and Bradley H. Short, "Branch Libraries and Discrete Collections," *ARL SPEC Kit* 255 (December 1999).

15. Ibid., 8.

16. Marjorie E. Murfin and Charles A. Bunge, "Paraprofessionals at the Reference Desk," *Journal of Academic Librarianship* 14, no. 1 (1988) 10-14.

17. Ibid., 11.

18. Ibid., 12.

19. Ibid.

20. Ibid.,13.

21. Ibid.,14.

22. Ibid.

23. Terry Rodgers, *The Library Paraprofessional: Notes from the Underground* (Jefferson, N.C.: McFarland, 1997).

24. Ibid., 164.

25. Ibid., 165.

26. Ibid., 166.

27. Nancy J. Emmick, "Nonprofessionals on Reference desks in Academic Libraries," *The Reference Librarian* 12 (1985) 149-160.

28. Ibid., 153.

29. Rodgers, 166.

30. Emmick, 155.

31. Rodgers, 166.

32. Emmick, 154.

33. Rodgers, 167-168.

34. Rodgers, passim.

35. Ibid., 168.

36. Ibid., 170.

37. Ibid., 171.

38. "Ask ARLIS IV: Training Paraprofessionals and Support Staff for Reference Work in the Art Library," *Art Documentation* (Summer 1992) 78-79 (session moderated by Patricia Lynagh and recorded by Eumie Imm).

39. Ibid., 78.

40. Ibid.

41. Ibid.

42. Ibid.

43. Ibid., 79.

APPENDIX A. Size of Collections Responding

Collection	Monographs	Current Periodical Subscriptions	Video/DVD	Slides	Other
1	19000	60	0	90000	0
2	75000	200	0	300000	5000 digital images
3	70000	200	1	115500	0
4	20000	110	20	0	0
5	150000	400	500	0	0
6	31000	210	100	0	0
7	86000	330	0	0	0
8	93000	150	165	0	125 cds
9	33000	100	120	0	0
10	23000	180	410	98000	1500 artist books
11	100000	300	0	250000	0
12	100000	300	100	325000	40000 mounted pictures
13	29000	210	0	0	0
14	74000	300	400	0	0
15	20000	100	225	0	0
16	175000	1000	50	0	15000 pamphlets
17	97000	350	500	0	0
18	32000	91	0	0	0
19	25000	110	0	0	0
20	82000	250	0	0	0
21	150000	220	10000	40	8000
22	70000	200	750	0	0
23	11000	30	100	0	0
24	69000	44	0	15000	42000 pamphlets and exhibit catalogs
25	39000	200	0	0	0
26	20000	80	35000	0	0
27	105000	460	600	0	0
28	25000	100	400	75000	blueprints, maps, etc.
29	15000	60	200	40000	
30	160000	492	344	198000	1000 photos, 119 computer files
31	75000	200	470	370000	0

APPENDIX B. Total Staff Full-Time Equivalent in Responding Libraries

Collection	Students* *many respondents gave total, not FTE	Lower Level Support Staff	Paraprofessional or Technical Staff	Visual Resources Professionals	MLS Librarians	Other
1	2	0	0	0	0.8	0
2	2.5	0	4	1	2	0
3	2.25	1	1	0	1	0
4	13 (shared)	1	1	0	1	0
5	13	0	2	0	1	0
6	2	1	1	0	1.5	0
7	15	0	3	0	1	0
8	2	0	1	0	1	0
9	6	0	2	0	1	0
10	3	0.5	1	1	2	0
11	1-15 per semester	0.3	0	1.5	2	0
12	15	2.5	2	1	11	0
13	15	0	3	0	1	0
14	0.9	0	1	0	1	0
15	0	0	3	0	0.3	0
16	4	0.5	1	0	0.82	0
17	0.5	1	2	0	2	0
18	8	0	1	0	1	0
19	2	2	1	0	1	0
20	2	0	1	0	1	0
21	10	0	5	0	5	2 interns
22	0	0	1	0	2	0
23	0	0	0	0	0.6	.2 volunteer
24	1	1	0	part time varies	1.5	0
25	2	1	0	0	1	0
26	6	1	0	0	1	0
27	12	5	0	0	4	0
28	10	1	1	1	4	0
29	1	0.2	1	0.2	0	0
30	3	0	3	1	2	0
31	2	0	1	1	1	0

Managing the Small Art Museum Library

Joan M. Benedetti

SUMMARY. Small art museum libraries are among the most administratively challenging of special libraries–and the most rewarding. Managing this most glamorous of research venues as the solo professional or
with minimal assistance inevitably tests the librarian's deepest personal
and professional reserves. He or she constantly weighs the desire to serve
a highly attractive clientele–curators, art educators, docents, collectors,
artists and independent researchers with the reality of what one librarian
can do. Technology has an enormous impact on libraries and on art historical research, but small libraries struggle to pay for it. Services are
possible today in small libraries that were available in only the largest institutions a decade ago. Although our OPACs can work "24/7," human
beings cannot. Solo art museum librarians love their jobs but are in constant danger of burn-out. By managing themselves, they will keep their
morale and their professional standards high. *[Article copies available for a
fee from The Haworth Document Delivery Service: 1-800-HAWORTH. E-mail address: <docdelivery@haworthpress.com> Website: <http://www.HaworthPress.com>
© 2003 by The Haworth Press, Inc. All rights reserved.]*

KEYWORDS. Small art museum libraries, solo librarians, one-person librarians, art museum library management, museum library management

Joan M. Benedetti was Cataloger, L.A. County Museum of Art Research Library at
the time this was written. She has recently retired. She was a solo librarian at The Craft
& Folk Art Museum in Los Angeles, 1976-1997, served from 1989-1994 as Director of
the Center for the Study of Art and Culture, an adjunct program of the CAFAM Research Library, and has been an active member of ARLIS/NA since 1977.

[Haworth co-indexing entry note]: "Managing the Small Art Museum Library." Benedetti, Joan M. Co-published simultaneously in *Journal of Library Administration* (The Haworth Information Press, an imprint of The
Haworth Press, Inc.) Vol. 39, No. 1, 2003, pp. 23-44; and: *The Twenty-First Century Art Librarian* (ed: Terrie L.
Wilson) The Haworth Information Press, an imprint of The Haworth Press, Inc., 2003, pp. 23-44. Single or multiple copies of this article are available for a fee from The Haworth Document Delivery Service
[1-800-HAWORTH, 9:00 a.m. - 5:00 p.m. (EST). E-mail address: docdelivery@haworthpress.com].

INTRODUCTION

There are museum libraries; there are art museum libraries. And then there are *small* art museum libraries. This paper looks primarily, though not exclusively, at art museum libraries run by "solo librarians."[1] Also known as "one-person librarians," or OPLs, it turns out these brave folks work in museums of many sizes, but the term refers to a situation in which they are "the only librarian (or only professional librarian) in a library or information center."[2]

For the past five years, I have worked as a cataloger in a large art research library in a large metropolitan survey museum, the Los Angeles County Museum of Art (LACMA). Before coming to work at LACMA, I was for 21 years the Museum Librarian at a much smaller, more specialized museum, the Craft & Folk Art Museum (CAFAM),[3] just across the street, but a world away in terms of funding and staffing.

Not surprisingly, my experience as a professional librarian in these two settings has been very different. In some ways, my experience at the large, fully staffed and supported library at LACMA has put my years as a one-person librarian at CAFAM into perspective, giving me an enhanced appreciation of the special qualities–and problems–of the small art museum library. I decided to seek out the experiences of others working in these settings, and to report here on the patterns and principles that might emerge.

WHAT IS A SMALL ART MUSEUM LIBRARY?

In March/April of 2002, as background research for this paper, I conducted a survey focusing on small art museum libraries, drawing on a volunteer sample from the membership of the Art Libraries Society of North America (ARLIS/NA), initially from the e-mail list of the Solo Librarians Discussion Group.[4] One of my underlying assumptions was that small museum libraries would be found in small museums. However, as survey data came in, it became clear that small museum libraries are not necessarily found in small museums, and some medium-sized and larger museums housed libraries staffed by solo librarians. Some of these were among the oldest museums in the United States and some of their libraries, if measured by collection size, could not be called "small libraries."[5] A few of the librarians in these facilities were the survivors of a larger professional staff that had recently been cut back; others have been solo librarians for a decade or more.

A recent article in *Museum News* (March/April 2002) written by Ron Chew,[6] Executive Director of the Wing Luke Asian Museum in Seattle, gave me a different perspective on the definition of "small" as it applies to museums:

> The exact number of small museums is unknown; the count varies according to the source. . . . According to the AAM [American Association of Museums] Small Museum Administrators Committee (SMAC), a small museum has a budget of less than $350,000. However, the federal Institute of Museum and Library Services sets the cut-off point at $250,000. . . . AAM estimates that there are more than 8,200 museums in the country, a majority of which can be considered small. . . . In the opinion of Roger Lidman, director of the Pueblo Grande Museum in Phoenix, "AAM is not on small museums' radar, and they are not on AAM's radar." He argues that there are nearly 16,000 museums in the country, most of which are small, far more than AAM accounts for. He bases this figure on a 1997 survey of state museum associations (summarized in a report that he co-authored called *Are Museums Ready for the Year 2000*, published by the Museum Association of Arizona).

Small museums are not alone in being ignored by the AAM; museum libraries are likewise "not on their radar," and they have long resisted the idea of including museum libraries among the facilities required of a museum for accreditation. This was noted in 1977, in an unpublished Master's Paper, written by Lynne Ann Waldruff[7] in partial fulfillment for a Master of Science in Library Science at the University of North Carolina at Chapel Hill:

> As directors cut budgets and staffs, the art museum library may feel particularly threatened because of the relative lack of importance that the museum profession has placed in its work. . . . In the checklist [*Museum Accreditation: Professional Standards*, 1973] utilized by the American Association of Museums visiting committee evaluating museums requesting accreditation, there are only three questions out of 170 involving the library and reference tools available. The library is not specifically mentioned as one of the main areas of concern. . . . An inadequate library has not been listed as a reason to table or reject accreditation of a museum.

Almost twenty years later, Esther Green Bierbaum reported the situation had changed very little:

> Documentary evidence suggests that the museum community itself gives museum libraries short shrift. For example, less space is given to the library in the American Association of Museums (AAM) accreditation standards than to any other facility or services. The 1992 AAM survey of 8,179 American museums included one question about library facilities, burying it in section E.57A, "Public Programs [*Museum Accreditation: A Handbook for the Institution*. Washington, D.C.: American Association of Museums, 1990]. The six questions of the institutional evaluation form (out of more than 100) that are directed to library facilities emphasize research support and collection organization. Museum libraries do not yet appear to be an overwhelming concern for the museum profession.[8]

This seeming reluctance by the AAM to give more than the most cursory acknowledgement to the value of museum libraries may not be rooted in a lack of respect for museum libraries per se. It may reflect more of a desire to encourage even the smallest museums to come under the AAM umbrella—or it may be that libraries are just "not on their radar." The reality of small museum life is that, for museums under a certain budgetary and staff size, the provision of professionally directed library services will not be possible unless the museum is lucky enough to find a professional librarian (perhaps retired) who is willing to volunteer. In this kind of marginal situation, the volunteer is not necessarily a "scab," taking a job that would otherwise be a paid position. If the volunteer professional is worth his or her salt, they will think creatively about how to steer the museum toward professional standards, utilizing interns from the local library school if possible, perhaps writing some grant proposals, possibly involving the museum in a library consortium, doing all they can to prepare the museum for hiring a professional librarian when its needs have outgrown a volunteer operation. Esther Green Bierbaum, in her second edition of *Museum Librarianship*[9] provides an excellent list of "Staffing Alternatives" when a museum cannot afford a full-time professional librarian. Her suggestions ensure that there will be input from a professional librarian even when one cannot be added to the permanent staff.

In all, then, the small art museum librarians (all ARLIS/NA members) who participated in my survey are mostly *not* from museums that would be considered small. I asked respondents to report not only their library's budget, but that of the parent organization as well. Although one-third of the respondents did not answer this question, of the two-thirds that did, only one worked in a museum whose budget was under $1,000,000. The median museum budget reported was $4,750,000 and the responses ranged from $500,000 to $25,000,000. Yet in all but two of these cases, these were libraries with one professional (or less) and no more than 1.50 support staff.

Small art museum libraries are among the most administratively challenging of art libraries–and the most rewarding–though not monetarily. Two respondents to the survey commented they would recommend it to "anyone who could afford it." Managing this most glamorous of research venues as the solo professional or with minimal assistance inevitably tests the librarian's deepest personal and professional reserves. Solo librarianship, once one has committed oneself to a particular venue, is usually a labor of love.[10] A professional librarian in a small art museum library weighs constantly the desire to serve a highly attractive clientele–which will include curators, museum educators, docents, artists, collectors, teachers, and independent scholars–with the reality of what one librarian, however energetic and highly trained, can do. A love of the subject matter and a respect for the clientele and the institution that employs them can ease the daily political, technical, personnel, and funding challenges of working in a small art museum library.

After working for five years in a large, fully supported library in a museum with over 50 departments, including 12 separate curatorial departments, I look back on my years as a solo librarian at the Craft & Folk Art Museum and see clearly that I miss most of all two things: being a part of almost everything that went on at CAFAM–or at least knowing about it; and being able to shape the collection and the programs of the CAFAM Library. A very important plus–for small libraries and for small museums–is the ability to see relatively quickly the results of your personal efforts. Working at CAFAM was a struggle, but those of us on the staff who persevered could see clearly where we wanted to go. In the long run, we achieved a remarkable amount of success–and we had a good deal of fun doing it.

WHAT'S SO SPECIAL ABOUT WORKING IN AN ART MUSEUM?

I would like to review some general aspects of the art museum as a library venue before focusing on the situation of the solo, or minimally-staffed art museum library. These are characteristics of almost all art museum libraries. For anyone whose primary subject interest is in art or art history, the very idea of working in an art museum is exciting. Librarians with art degrees are no different, and most of the art museum librarians who participated in my survey responded with enthusiasm to questions about art museums as places to work. In response to the question, "What is distinctive about working in an art museum library?" here are some typical comments:

- You are always surrounded by art, which feeds you even when the work is overwhelming.
- I like working closely with curators to have a sense of what is going on in the museum world in general through my work in the library.
- Close involvement with other areas of the museum, opportunities to interact with artists and curators, immersion in subject matter I'm passionate about.

There are two major characteristics of art museums that set their libraries apart from other art libraries. The first is related to the purpose of museums, which (according to the AAM *Professional Standards for Accreditation*, 1989) is "essentially educational or aesthetic . . . and to own and utilize tangible objects, care for them, and exhibit them to the public on some regular schedule."[11] The primary purpose of the museum library, therefore, is to support research concerning the museum's objects, as well as those it may not own but exhibits, by providing information on those and related objects as well as pertinent information on their cultural context, and the creators of those objects. Related to the support of the museum's objects (usually referred to as "the permanent collection") may be provision of images of those objects, and provision of information (usually through auction catalogs) about their purchase.

It is important to remember that no matter how many other functions the library may take on (supporting docents and education programs, archiving museum historical documents,[12] serving independent scholars and other members of the public), the *primary* justification for the art museum library collection is support of the museum's object collections and/or its exhibition programs. This focus justifies the library's existence in many ways: Even if the museum staff, for example, is relatively small, a library collection commensurate with its object collections in size and depth is appropriate. Because it is a research library, it will weed its collection very little; the bibliographic history of the museum's objects and their cultural context will likely grow in value with age. Of course, at the same time that one builds the library collection to reflect the collecting and exhibiting program of the museum, some attention must be paid to what Anna Dvořák at the North Carolina Museum of Art calls "the slow, purposeful development of a high-quality research facility."[13] This would include development of "the reference collection and other valuable research resources which the library will not be able to afford once they are out of print. This category includes *catalogues raisonnes* of important artists . . . and other titles which are out of proportion to the library budget, but of indisputable importance."[14]

Placing the mission of the library directly in support of the museum's object collection and exhibitions makes it an integral part of the museum's operation, and keeps it in close collaboration with its primary clients, the curators. The curatorial function is the second major characteristic of art museums that sets their libraries apart from other art libraries. In a classic essay on the subject of how "The Art Museum Library Serves the Curator," Grace McCann Morley, then Curator, Cincinnati Art Museum, wrote in 1933:

> . . . *as a direct aid in all study and research, the museum library is absolutely indispensable to the curator.* On its resources he must depend for the careful preparation and documentation that are the groundwork and background of all museum work. . . . *from the curator's point of view the library is the very heart of the museum.* It is the repository of his most indispensable tools. Books stand next in importance to the art works themselves in the operation of any Art museum. Without their help, the systematic arrangement, and complete identification of art objects proper to museum display and study collections would be impossible, for this work is done according to the accumulated knowledge and experience of a fellowship of scholars past and present, whose findings are available to all in printed form. The library is the coordinating, organizing, and preservative agency, as well as the active seeker of knowledge, through which the curator can tap without unnecessary loss of time and energy the numberless sources of information. . . . For its work the Art museum library deserves recognition and every facility that can add to the realization of its ideal of efficiency. Above all *it deserves an adequate staff to perform the exacting tasks set it.* [Italics added][15]

Lucky the art museum librarian who has even one curator so articulate in their appreciation! Curators may sometimes take their museum libraries for granted, but they will normally be people with research experience as well as museum experience, and the more research experience they have, the more they will naturally tend to support the library. They will not be very demanding in terms of reference queries; they will usually know exactly what publications they want. For this reason, they will be supporters of increased acquisitions budgets. If budgets are limited, they will want to make extensive use of interlibrary loan.

However, even curators will not always understand the *operation* of the library. It becomes extremely important, therefore, for the museum librarian to encourage the museum staff to become invested in the value of the library. They become invested as they discover it, use it, and see its potential to make their work more efficient. New curators (and other new staff) should be invited to tour the library and see some of the special collections, get instruction on use of the OPAC, how to order ILLs, routing of periodicals, and other special staff services. The museum librarian should attend all general staff meetings and take every opportunity to informally advertise library collections and services as they relate to museum collections and projects. If possible, they should also attend curatorial meetings so that they can stay ahead of curatorial concerns and matters related to the object collections and exhibitions.

Curators and art librarians are natural allies, and a librarian's education and activities should reflect that. In addition to the library degree, art museum librarians should have either an undergraduate or second master's degree in art history.[16] They should be active in professional organizations, writing papers and giving presentations. They should also consider joining organizations outside of the library profession, such as the AAM or one of its regional affiliates, or the CAA (the College Art Association), if for no other reason than to receive their publications, which will keep them aware of issues important to museum staff. When those organizations have meetings nearby, the librarian should consider going. As noted above, the AAM, in particular, could benefit from a more visible librarian membership. In any case, the librarian's interest and enthusiasm for the museum collection, its exhibitions, and other projects preoccupying the museum staff should be a reflection of a collegial situation. If possible, the museum librarian should report to the director of the museum without an intermediary. The library department should be seen as equal to other museum departments, such as education or curatorial. If this kind of access to the director is not possible, the library should be under the umbrella of the museum department that does the most research concerning the museum's objects and/or exhibitions, which is usually the curatorial department. The librarian's supervisor should, in any case, be someone in a position of power in the museum, who values the library.

In museum venues (as in most special libraries), the librarian's supervisor will not be a librarian. This situation is not all bad: A curator or museum administrator will be likely to bow to the librarian's expertise concerning internal library procedures. They will be bottom-line oriented, wanting the library to run smoothly and efficiently and to meet the needs of its clientele. It may, of course, be more difficult to explain to them an operational need (justifying new technology, for example). A way must be found to talk about what happens in the library in a way that museum professionals can understand. For example, avoid library jargon. A librarian is a kind of curator: Talk about collections and access, visitors and users–not "patrons." This will put the library in the same domain as the museum.

Trust must also be developed between the library and the museum staff. Much of the information about museum collections and exhibitions is proprietary. Art museums are blatantly competitive with each other in terms of collection building, funding, and programming. Although collaborative projects between art museums are more common now than they once were, they are still the exception. There are also issues of privacy when it comes to dealing with potential donors to the museum, especially donors of objects. The art museum librarian (who has been taught in library school the importance of *sharing* information) must know when to be discreet in providing information to researchers who are not on the museum staff. If the librarian is not seen as trustworthy, they will certainly not be allowed into curatorial meetings, and they won't gain the respect of non-librarian colleagues on the museum staff.

The museum librarian would do well to realize that there are aspects of "show business" to museum business. This is seen most obviously in the mounting of special exhibitions and the media "blitz" that accompanies the occasional blockbuster. But all exhibitions have theatrical parallels. The gallery is a kind of theater and great attention is paid to the design of the space, the choice of colors, the flow of one "scene" into another, the lighting, and the "script" (the label copy or audio tour). Exhibitions have opening nights (perhaps more than one), an exhibition has a "run," then is "dark" while a new "show" is mounted. Media reviews of exhibitions can make a big difference in museum attendance and, therefore, in museum revenues. An appreciation for this situation will heighten one's sense of being part of the museum "ensemble."

To the media and the public, the artists are usually the stars, especially if they are living artists. But inside the museum–and, for colleagues at related museums as well–the curator will probably be a star, especially if they have an established track record of mounting successful exhibitions or of attracting stellar donations. The curator has star status because they possess the most direct power *vis à vis* the museum's primary mission: to "own and utilize tangible objects." In a collecting museum, the curator researches and recommends objects for purchase, and researches and proposes exhibition ideas, writes the catalogs, oversees exhibition installations, and in general, holds sway within all but the largest of art museums. That the librarian can be a colleague of these heavenly creatures may sometimes seem impossible, but it is important that museum librarians refrain from becoming either star-struck or intimidated. Good, efficient bibliographic assistance to curators (as to *all* museum staff) in an atmosphere of collegial service to the museum is what is needed. Although the museum environment can sometimes be politically charged–and the librarian must not be politically naïve–the goal must be to stay out of political storms in order to best serve the museum as a whole for the long run.

There are many ways to establish collegial rapport between the librarian and museum staff. In all but the largest museums, opportunities abound for librarians to become involved in projects and events outside of the library and outside of their role as librarian. If one is a good writer or editor, one might involve oneself in the museum's publications. If one has design or carpentry skills, one might help with exhibition installations. If one has good ideas and good relations with the director in a museum with a small curatorial staff, one might even occasionally be able to curate an exhibition or at least act as a producer (hiring an outside curator). Frequently, librarians volunteer or are called upon to act as information services coordinator, setting up various computer systems for the museum or developing the museum's website.

All of these things can be very tempting–especially if one is paid for them–but beware: They are inherently dangerous for a solo librarian or one that has a very small staff. Because these non-library tasks are much more visible–even glamorous–than day-to-day library work, it is possible that they will start to take priority. The best solution is to do these things outside of library hours. The calling of librarianship is demanding and in a small library must remain the main priority.

THE CURRENT LITERATURE ON ART MUSEUM LIBRARIES

Considering that a majority of art librarians have at least one degree in art history (in addition to their library school degree) and considering the centrality of art museums to the study of art history, it is somewhat surprising that so little has been written specifically on the subject of art museum libraries. Lynne Ann Waldruff commented on this in her Master's Paper written 25 years ago;[17] why is the state of the literature so little improved since then?

In the last 15 years, less than a dozen or so articles have been written on the topic of art museum libraries; of those, most were either histories of individual libraries, or focused on one aspect of service or collections. Only one overview has appeared, the brief, but well-articulated *Art Documentation* article by Anna Dvořák cited earlier. That piece, as well as the essay by the curator, Grace McCann Morley, whose "love letter" to librarians was quoted previously, deserve to be reprinted in a compilation devoted to art museum libraries. Monographs exist on art libraries (though surprisingly few), museum libraries, special libraries, and even a few on small museum libraries, but I could find only *one* published monograph devoted to art museum libraries, and it is strictly a bibliographic list that includes no commentary.[18] In addition, there is the above-mentioned unpublished, but well-written, 1977 Master's Paper based on a survey by Lynne Ann Waldruff.

Perhaps even more striking is the absence of discussion on the specific characteristics of art museum libraries *within the few general texts on art librarianship.* Lois Swan Jones' *Art Libraries and Information Services* (Orlando, FL: Academic Pr., 1986) is the only one that includes a section on "Kinds of Art Libraries." One and one-half pages in this section are devoted to art museum libraries. Both sets of ARLIS/NA *Standards*[19] have sections devoted to art museum libraries. *Facilities Standards for Art Libraries and Visual Resources Collections*, compiled by ARLIS members and edited by Betty Jo Irvine[20] includes statistics related to art museum libraries. The others assume that information about art libraries in general will be sufficient no matter what the venue, and they tend to stress collection development matters and, to a lesser degree, organization of the collection, rather than issues related to the specialized clientele, purposes, and problems of art museum libraries. For more pertinent information, one can turn to the literature on special libraries and museum libraries, but so far these publications have not been written by art librarians and assume a greater availability of literature on art museum libraries than is actually the case.[21] Several books on museum careers include sections on the museum librarian.[22]

Of course, the more general literature is helpful, especially that published by ARLIS/NA, ARLIS/UK, and the SLA (Special Libraries Association). The growing body of work on the so-called "OPL" is also of special value to the solo librarian.[23] But in all, the body of literature on art museum libraries remains inadequate. This may be because the population of art museum librarians is small in proportion to art librarianship as a whole, though in ARLIS/NA, the Museum Library Division is one of the largest (over 250 members); only the Academic Libraries Division (over 300) is larger. I suspect the dearth of art museum library literature is mainly because art museum librarians have less time than their academic counterparts to devote to extracurricular tasks like professional writing. It doesn't help that art librarianship is taught at only a few library schools, and that the pay scale in museums is lower than that of academic art libraries.[24] Also, some academic librarians face "publish or perish" ultimatums in regard to tenure. This motivation doesn't exist for most museum librarians.

WORKING IN THE SMALL ART MUSEUM LIBRARY

The great thing about the solo or small art museum library job is that you get to do everything. The awful thing about the solo or small art museum library job is that you *have* to do everything. Solo librarians may be exhausted, but they are never bored. If they tire of doing one sort of thing, selecting or ordering books for instance, they can easily and with complete justification, switch to something else, such as going over the serials subscription list, writing up volunteer job descriptions, training a volunteer or an intern, sorting some exhibition slides, preparing a docent reserve shelf, answering a reference query, working on the budget, helping the curator who needed their materials "yesterday," finishing the grant proposal whose deadline is Friday, or working on the cataloging, the backlog of which only grows bigger. Management as a solo librarian essentially means managing yourself.

Besides the usual professional tasks, there are other jobs the solo librarian gets to do that one doesn't hear about in library school: shifting books, packing up interlibrary loan requests, checking out books, reshelving, refiling, even, occasionally, sweeping and vacuuming. One survey respondent said, "Don't plan on keeping your hands clean; there's lots of active work to do in the small staff library!"

Why, in spite of all this, and in spite of relatively low salaries and low budgets, in spite of running out of space, in spite of a substantial amount of job insecurity, did so many art museum librarians confess in the survey that they "just love" their jobs? Here are a few answers to the survey question, "Would you recommend working in a small art museum library to another librarian?":

- Yes, I have freedom to structure my time as I see fit; opportunity to work closely with the larger organization.
- Yes! This is a fascinating job that I personally find highly rewarding. The duties here utilize many skills learned in the various other jobs I have held; this is equivalent to running your own small business. Also due to the small staff size, many more menial tasks have to be performed.
- Absolutely! But someone with lots of LIBRARY experience, not just art history experience. Failed art historians do not successful librarians make, in my opinion. And you really have to know your (library) stuff to hold your own with the PhDs. Being the only library professional in a sea of other types of professionals, I have to not only explain what it is I do, but why I am doing it.
- The clientele is well-educated, very polite, and quite appreciative.

Of course, not everyone was so positive. Here are some more cautious comments:

- If you can afford to work in a small art museum library, I'd recommend it.
- I would have to think long and hard about it. Our museum is very volatile financially and the library has usually been the target of staff cutbacks when we are struggling financially. It is not a very stable situation.

When asked "What special qualities are required of the librarian in a small art museum library?" words like "flexibility" and "stamina" were most often mentioned:

- Ability to represent the library to everyone–the public, museum staff, and other librarians. The ability to handle budgets, human resource issues, and other administrative tasks in addition to traditional library skills.
- Subject knowledge; fondness for the subject; personal involvement with some aspect of the subject. And for a one-person library: strength, stamina, and great determination!
- Must be self-directed; able to work alone much of the time, yet able to collaborate with other museum staff. Must be resourceful, both

with research and with limited budgets. Must be good at managing your time and your work. Must be able to direct volunteer staff.
- Ability to juggle many responsibilities and tasks; diplomacy; ability to focus on long-term goals.
- Patience; flexibility; political savvy.
- Subject knowledge a dead heat with advocacy skills–the ability to make the library a well-used resource.
- You must have the initiative to start a project and the resolve to follow through and actually get it done. The only pressure I have to "get things done" most of the time comes from myself. Therefore, creating a new initiative is not enough; you must also be a self-motivator to keep the momentum going.
- You've got to learn to deal with some pretty high maintenance patrons–diplomacy and good manners are a requirement!
- Flexibility, strong organizational ability, and an abundant amount of energy.
- Courage!

As is clear from these comments, working in a small art museum library takes an essentially entrepreneurial spirit. It means always being pro-active and assertive in service to your museum, assessing a need, figuring out a solution, and going for it–with the blessing, of course, of your supervisor, if it is something that will affect anyone outside the library. It is wonderful to be able to go directly to an office supply store, or a library catalog, and get what you need immediately, rather than putting in an order to a purchasing department and waiting a week or more. It is not so wonderful to pay for things out of your own pocket and worry about how soon–or whether or not–you will be reimbursed. But for the creative individual who "can afford it" and has "an abundant amount of energy," seeing your ideas in action relatively quickly can be very rewarding in all but financial terms.

And speaking of money, even a one-person library needs it, and what librarians sometimes forget is that you have to *ask* for it. Just because it hasn't been given to you, doesn't mean it is not available. One survey respondent did not know she even *had* a budget as such until the survey motivated her to ask. This is where the librarian's relationship with the museum's director (or other supervisor) is critical. Budgeting is normally a process of give and take and the library must compete with other museum departments. Our best argument in the financial battle is that the library supports the museum as a *whole*, and this is the concept–with back-up statistics–that will best justify a realistic budget request. But since you may have to give as well as get, you must have a good idea of what your priorities are: what is indispensable, what can be negotiated, and what can be postponed, if necessary.

In preparing for budget meetings, think about the library in the context of the museum as a whole. What is the total museum budget as compared to the library budget? What is the total museum staff as compared to the library staff? In many cases, the museum budget and staffing are huge in comparison to that of the library. Is the staff size of the education department or the curatorial department very much larger than that of the library? Perhaps you can make the administration see the inequity. However, you can do this only if they can see the benefits clearly. Highlight the budgetary items that contribute most directly to the quality of life of the museum staff: routing journals, doing interlibrary loans, getting the library catalog online so that it's available from every staff member's desktop; providing scanned images from the museum's collection; providing subscriptions to databases–if you can afford them or get them through a consortium arrangement. Make sure you are valuing the library's services appropriately within the context of the museum as a whole. If you don't believe in what you are doing, you won't be able to convince anyone else.

The library must be seen not only as the excellent research collection and service that it is–or could be; it must also be seen as contributing to the positive, serious *image* of the museum. Remind the administration of how great it is to be able to show off the library to V.I.P. visitors. (Or how great it *would* be if the library had the new shelving or the renovation that is needed.) Though the museum library primarily serves the museum staff, it can be useful for museum public relations as well. Have you been keeping those statistics? Remember, record and communicate to the administration the number of requests for information that have come into the museum and have been referred to the library instead of bothering the administration or the curators. Many of the calls we answered at the Craft & Folk Art Museum Library came from people who had called the general museum number, not having had the faintest idea that the museum had a library. Save your more interesting e-reference questions and include them in your annual report. Solicit "love letters" from the patrons for whom you have performed some out-of-the-ordinary services. (You'll also need them to include in any grant proposals that you write.) Remember that sometimes what is simplest for us is extremely impressive to a research novice. Sometimes those novices are on the museum staff–they may even be administrators!

SMALL ART MUSEUM LIBRARIES IN THE 21ST CENTURY– IT'S THE TECHNOLOGY, STUPID!

Technology has had an enormous impact on libraries and on art historical research. Ease of distribution and manipulation of images and text have made services possible today in smaller libraries that were available in only the largest institutions a decade ago. But it has taken a while for the benefits to trickle down to small museum libraries. Although computers have been in use in large libraries for much longer than they have been in use in all but the largest museums, it is only within the last few years, with the widespread use of the Internet and the World Wide Web, and lower prices of hardware and software, that computers have become commonplace in small museum libraries. Scholars in museums, just like scholars in academia, have had a long computer learning curve. Most of us working in museum libraries today still spend some portion of almost every day teaching staff and docents to use the computer catalog.

The computer was supposed to save time, but in libraries–as elsewhere–we are continuously surprised by how much busier we are now than in years past. A large part of the problem is that technology has made it possible to do a lot more. We expect (and are expected by our administrators) to do much more in 24 hours than was even dreamed of 10-15 years ago. If we have computers at home–and most of us do–it becomes even harder to draw the line between the job and private life. Our OPAC may be available "24/7," but the people working in the small art museum library cannot be–even if they were to give up their personal lives. Setting priorities is still a human job–and more important than ever.

Although the overall cost of technology is going down, it is a relatively new part of the budget for many small libraries. Most libraries have had separate budget lines for computer services, but some are now re-thinking this. Perhaps database subscriptions should be an acquisitions item. Some very good news is that all of my survey respondents have at least one computer in their libraries with Internet access; some have many more. The ability to access listservs such as ARLIS-L and the ARLIS/NA website has had a very positive effect on the solo librarian's morale, to say nothing of their ability to do reference or to catalog. Solo librarians can now be in touch with any number of listservs or individual colleagues, no matter how distant, instantly and at no cost, to get online advice about virtually anything–vendors, equipment, security issues, copyright, OPAC software–or any number of traditional librarianship issues. The ARLIS-L archive, accessible from the ARLIS/NA website <www.arlisna.org>, is a treasure-store of professional information.

Most of my survey respondents had only recently purchased or installed OPAC software; some are still in the process of deciding what to buy. All who have (or will soon have) OPACs are planning for them to be available on museum staff desktops and ultimately on the web. Some have already accomplished this. A wide range of OPAC software products are in use. Of 20 respondents who have or who are planning to buy OPAC software, 16 different programs were reported. Some who have not been able to afford OPAC software and subscriptions to cataloging utilities have come up with ingenious methods of utilizing the Internet and word processing or spreadsheet software to create home-grown computer catalogs. Several libraries acquired their OPACs as part of a consortium contract. All who participated in the survey use their computer to achieve some level of automation for reference or acquisitions or for obtaining catalog copy, even though they may still be filing catalog cards.

Eighteen of 34 of survey respondents have frozen both their manual catalogs and shelflist card files–or never had either. Three plan to freeze both when all their records are transferred to their OPAC. Five have frozen their catalog, but keep their shelflist in card form. Eight are maintaining all their card files. Now that the Library of Congress and most major research libraries in the world have their catalogs on the web, it is relatively easy to copy a catalog from these sources instead of subscribing to OCLC or RLIN. This practice has a down-side, however, as many non-L.C. records are non-standard or of dubious quality. And of course, having to re-key information, or even cutting and pasting, is much more time-consuming and error-prone, than batch-downloading from a cataloging utility. In some cases, the inability to move forward with automation may simply be inertia brought on by solo librarian overload. It takes time to do the research necessary to project costs and analyze benefits. OCLC and RLIN both offer many economic options. The benefits are amazing and–once your system is in place–quite cost-efficient–especially if you are willing to stop buying or typing and filing cards.

Grants are available at least for the initial phases of library automation. Museum administrators like the idea of making museum library catalogs available on the web–once they get beyond the cost of digitizing records. It is another attractive web service the museum can offer–and it is publicity for the museum as well! Another possible option is to join a local consortium. Consortium members who get cataloging free (or for a modest fee) in exchange for access to their catalog records were among the happiest of the survey respondents.

What is becoming universally understood is that with the new accessibility of library catalogs on the web, standards are now more important than ever.[25] The importance of the MARC format cannot be over-estimated. Librarians who purchase OPAC software (or construct local catalogs using database software) that cannot create MARC records are borrowing from Peter to pay Paul. All of those non-MARC records will have to be converted at some point in the future, in some cases, re-keyed. Don't forget a basic tenet of automation: If your system is well-designed, it allows you to never have to repeat yourself–and that includes never having to correct mistakes more than once. Automated records are more accurate records. But the solo librarian must be realistic. Consider this from *The Best of OPL II*:

> ... we should dispel the myth that using MARC necessarily means using full MARC records. The key to MARC is the tagging of fields, which makes it possible for the data in specific fields to be easily recognized and transferred from one database to another. Bibliographic records are broken down into dozens of fields and subfields, but the fact that MARC permits such a high level of specificity doesn't mean that it requires it.[26]

Equal in importance to the use of the MARC format is the use of standard authority files. For most art libraries, this means use of the Library of Congress Name Authorities and Subject Headings. This has not been easy for small libraries because LC authority files have been available only by subscription through a cataloging utility such as OCLC or RLIN and, as has been mentioned, libraries with relatively small budgets have been slow to take advantage of these services. Authority records contain much more than the authorized form of a name or subject heading. They also include essential cross-references as well as additional information helpful in determining the correct name or best choice of subject heading.[27]

My experience of transferring records from CAFAM's OPAC to LACMA's is instructive. The CAFAM OPAC software, though modest in price, had allowed me to download and create MARC records. These were easily converted and transferred to LACMA's OPAC; however, the CAFAM OPAC software did *not* allow me to download LC authority records, and it had no alternative way of providing cross-references. Provision of cross-references is especially important in special libraries that must use some alternative vocabularies, as I did in the CAFAM library because the terminology of craft and folk art is so problematic. (For example, LC still uses "handicraft," which is anathema to any serious craft artist.) At CAFAM, I had created a Rube Goldberg system of cross-references by adding them as 690s (local subject) to catalog records. Now I am having to correct many of the CAFAM records to bring them into conformity with the LC and AAT standards used by LACMA.

As of July 1, 2002, the Library of Congress has enabled searching of both its name and subject authority files free of charge on a trial basis. This is a monumental, historic step in the creation of an equitable cataloging environment, friendly to less wealthy libraries and supportive of national standards for libraries of all sizes. The next–and equally important–step toward equity must be the availability of affordable OPAC systems, compatible with all basic standards, so that all libraries and users can participate fully in the benefits of 21st century technology.

THERE ARE NO SMALL ART LIBRARIANS . . .

Librarians working in small art libraries, regardless of budgets, need to start thinking big. The Internet and the World Wide Web make this more possible than ever before. Think of the importance of your museum and how it deserves better, more accessible documentation. Think of the value of your library collections and how their cataloging records should be shared with other libraries–and with researchers far from where your museum is located. Even though you can't afford all the technology you need now, you deserve to be heard. You can participate with your professional colleagues online, if not in person, to lobby for more affordable cataloging tools, bibliographic indexes, and other databases.

Think creatively–and cooperatively. If a consortium doesn't exist in your region, perhaps you can start one on a small scale with a local college or art school. Above all, join with other art librarians in your area: in ARLIS/NA, in SLA, or in ALA. Attendance at professional meetings is not only good for you and good for your library, it's excellent publicity for your museum. Use your interlibrary loan system–or your acquisitions budget–to borrow or purchase some of the professional literature cited here or elsewhere in this volume. Think like an entrepreneur. If your museum won't pay for professional memberships or give you travel funds to attend meetings, you may need to use some personal funds, if you can possibly afford it, as a professional investment in yourself. Don't forget–travel awards are available (and sometimes go begging) from ARLIS/NA and SLA. You need all the help you can get–to make the job you have better–or to look for a better job. Your art museum librarian colleagues will be glad to help you. Don't hesitate to ask.

NOTES

1. This study was inspired and encouraged by members of the Art Libraries Society of North America (ARLIS/NA) Solo Librarians Discussion Group, led by Eumie Imm-Stroukoff, Librarian at the Georgia O'Keeffe Museum in Santa Fe. I am especially indebted to Eumie for her assistance and advice during the course of preparing the survey. Ken Soehner, Head, Watson Library, Metropolitan Museum of Art, and Immediate Past Chair, ARLIS/NA Museum Libraries Division, was also very supportive. I want to acknowledge the help of LACMA staff: Head Librarian, Deborah Barlow Smedstad, for her keen copyediting eye and substantive suggestions and Program Specialist Anne Diederick for her interlibrary loan skills.

2. Judith A. Siess, *The OPL Sourcebook: A Guide for Solo and Small Libraries.* (Medford, NJ: Information Today, Inc., 2001): 1. Seiss credits Guy St. Clair, who founded *The One-Person Librarian* newsletter, with invention of the term "one-person librarian," when he used it as the title of a discussion he led at the 1972 Special Libraries Association conference in Boston. Seiss took over publication of *The One-Person Librarian* (now called *The One-Person Library: A Newsletter for Librarians and Management*) in 1998.

3. The Craft & Folk Art Museum closed at the end of 1997 and its object collections were sold at auction at Butterfield & Butterfield Fine Art Auctioneers, Los Angeles. Its library was given to the L.A. County Museum of Art Research Library (LACMA paid for the cost of the move) and its archives were given to UCLA's Arts Special Collections. CAFAM reopened under the auspices of the City of L.A. Cultural Affairs Department in 1999. A short history of CAFAM and a description of its library collections can be found on the LACMA website *www.lacma.org*. Click on "Library/Research" and then on "Edith R. Wyle Craft & Folk Art Museum Library."

4. The survey form was sent to 30 museum librarian members of the Art Libraries Society of North America (ARLIS/NA) Solo Librarians Discussion Group and then to 20 additional museum librarians who responded to an announcement posted on the ARLIS/NA listserv. Of 50 forms distributed, 34 (68%) were returned. The survey results can be obtained by emailing the author at: benedetti4@adelphia.net. I wish to thank the following suvey participants, who gave me permission to use their names: Debby Aframe, Anna Brooke, Lynda Bunting, Mary Carpenter, Lois Crane, Sam Duncan, Lu Harper, Phil Heagy, Genni Houlihan, Eumie Imm-Stroukoff, Regina Kammer, Maryann Kempthorne, Mary E. Mallia, Sally McKay, James Mitchell, Mary Morman-Graham, Melisa Nicoud, Patrice O'Donoghue, William A. Peniston, Kristen Regina, Karen Schneider, Cheryl Siegel, Maurya Smith, Jim Soe Nyun, Kathleen Stacey, Rebecca D. Steel, Heather R. Stuart, Sharon Wasserman, Matt Wiggins, Cary Wilkins, and Tom Young. Three others asked to remain anonymous.

5. *Standards for Art Libraries and Fine Arts Slide Collections, Occasional Papers No. 2* (Tucson, AZ: Art Libraries Society of North America, 1983) includes definitions of "small," "medium," and "large" art libraries which, though somewhat arbitrary,

were useful for the purposes of this study. For art museum library collections, "small" is defined as "up to 20,000 volumes"; "medium" as "20,000 to 80,000 volumes"; and "large" as "over 80,000 volumes." A later ARLIS/NA publication, *Staffing Standards for Art Libraries and Visual Resources Collections* (Raleigh, NC, 1996), which largely supersedes the 1983 *Standards* doesn't include definitions.

6. Ron Chew, "In Praise of the Small Museum," *Museum News* 81:2 (March/April 2002): 36-41.

7. Lynne Ann Waldruff, "Art Museum Libraries: Functions and Priorities," Master's Paper for the M.S. in L.S. degree, August 1977, Chapel Hill, NC: University of North Carolina: 1-2.

8. Esther Green Bierbaum, "Museum Libraries: The More Things Change . . ." *Special Libraries* 87: 2 (Spring 1996): 74-75. This article was based on a 1994-95 survey done by Bierbaum of museum libraries randomly selected from the AAM's *Official Museum Directory*, 1994.

9. Esther Green Bierbaum, *Museum Librarianship, 2nd ed.* (Jefferson, NC: McFarland & Co., 2000): 79-81.

10. Sixteen (47%) of the 34 "Small Art Museum Libraries" survey respondents have held their present positions for over five years; of these, 12 (35%) have been at the same job for over 10 years and five of these (14.7%) have over 20 years' tenure. On the other hand, 18 respondents (53%) have held the same position for less than four years and half of these (27.5%) have worked in their present position for less than two years, suggesting a relatively high rate of turnover until a librarian has held a position for more than four years.

11. Quoted in *Museum Librarianship*, p. 163.

12. Twenty-one survey respondents, or roughly 2/3 of those surveyed, have responsibility for their institution's archives. Although librarians are not usually trained as archivists in library school, we often take on this job and train ourselves through reading or taking workshops offered by ARLIS/NA or SAA (the Society of American Archivists). The task of collecting contemporary institutional materials, especially in a small museum, is relatively easy. As queries to the library often concern past exhibitions, it is useful to have these files close at hand. An article written by Maureen Melton, archivist at the Museum of Fine Arts, Boston, "Preserving Love's Labors in the Museum Archives," *Art Documentation* 15 (1996): 1, 7-9, is informative and entertaining.

13. Anna Dvořák, "Small and Medium-Sized Art Museum Libraries: The Problems of Interdependence and Independence," *Art Documentation* 8: 2 (Summer 1989): 84.

14. Ibid.

15. *Special Libraries*, May 1933, 86-88; reprinted in: *A Reader in Art Librarianship (IFLA Publications 34)*, ed. Philip Pacey (NY: K.G. Saur, 1977): 48-50.

16. *ARLIS/NA Salary Survey 1990* (Tucson, AZ: ARLIS/NA, 1991): 12. Of 324 respondents to this 1990 survey, 65.4% reported "holding an art or art history degree." See also Dvořák, loc. cit.

17. Waldruff: 2-3.

18. Lucy D. Tuckerman, *Suggestions for the Library of a Small Museum of Art* (Washington, D.C.: American Association of Museums, 1928). Tuckerman's bibliography is based on the collection of the Worcester Art Museum Library, where she was the Librarian.

19. *Standards for Art Libraries and Fine Arts Slide Collections: Occasional Papers No. 2.* (Tucson, AZ: Art Libraries Society of North America, 1983); *Staffing Standards for Art Libraries and Visual Resources Collections: Occasional Paper No. 11.* (Raleigh, NC: Art Libraries Society of North America, 1996).

20. Englewood, CO: Libraries Unlimited, 1991.

21. *Museum Librarianship*: 2. An older work, but still useful, is a different publication with the same title, *Museum Librarianship*, a compilation of essays edited by John C. Larsen (Hamden, CT: Shoe String Press, 1985); three of the nine essays and the preface are written by art museum librarians, but the text is general with discussion of specific types of museum libraries avoided.

22. William A. Burns' *Your Future in Museums, Rev. ed.* (NY: R. Rosen Pr., 1967): 79-83, is a good overview, but needs to be updated; a more up-to-date but shorter discussion can be found in *Museums: A Place to Work; Planning Museum Careers*, by Jane R. Glaser with Artemis A. Zenetou (NY: Routledge, 1996): 104-105; *Museum Careers and Training: A Professional Guide*, by Victor J. Danilov (Westport, CT: Greenwood Press, 1994) includes multiple references to librarians, archivists, and preservationists and is a very thorough guide to museum careers, including salaries and training programs.

23. Judith Seiss' book, *The OPL Sourcebook*, cited above, is a goldmine of resource information on publications, organizations, websites, and listservs of special interest to solo librarians. Two excellent compilations, both full of practical advice, tips, and inspirational words, are *The Best of OPL: Five Years of the One-Person Library*, ed. Andrew Berner and Guy St. Clair (Washington, D.C.: Special Libraries Association, 1990) and *The Best of OPL II: Selected Reading from The One-Person Library, 1989-1994*, ed. Andrew Berner and Guy St. Clair (Washington, D.C.: Special Libraries Association, 1996).

24. *ARLIS/NA Salary Survey 1990*: 8-9. In comparing all respondents and in comparing only respondents working with "primarily traditional collections," academic salaries were substantially higher than those of museum staff. However, it is interesting to note that when respondents who were responsible for "primarily visual collections" were compared to those responsible for "primarily traditional collections," this difference disappeared; in fact salaries of museum staff working with primarily visual collections as compared to academic staff working with primarily visual collections were the same or slightly higher than their academic colleagues.

25. A relatively recent publication, *Special Libraries: A Cataloging Guide*, ed. Sheila S. Intner and Jean Weihs (Englewood, CO: Libraries Unlimited, Inc., 1998) is a substantial cataloging text that I wish had been available when I was working at CAFAM. It includes sections on LCSH and authority files, LCC and DDC, AACR2R and MARC, serials and series, extensive bibliographies and even cataloging exercises. Several chapters are devoted to specific types of special libraries, including "Cataloging in Art Libraries," by Amy Lucker, Librarian, Museum of Fine Arts, Boston. Two other very good art cataloging articles are "Some Comments on the Cataloging of Exhibition Catalogues, or, Who Was the Author of That Exhibition?" by Daniel Starr, Museum of Modern Art, *Art Documentation*: 15 (1996): 11-16, and "The Rules Have Changed: Library of Congress Subject Headings for Art and Architecture," by Amy E. Trendler, The Art Institute of Chicago, *Art Documentation*: 20, 2 (Fall 2001): 24-29.

26. *The Best of OPL II*, p. 25.

27. An excellent new text on authority work that will be of use to anyone working with authority files is *Maxwell's Guide to Authority Work*, by Robert L. Maxwell (Chicago: American Library Association, 2002).

MANAGING AND SERVICING COLLECTIONS IN AN ART AND ARCHITECTURE ENVIRONMENT

Integrating the Digitization of Visual Resources into Library Operations

Paula Hardin

SUMMARY. There are many issues involved in implementing digital library development and many decisions to be made. Integrating digitization as a routine component of visual resources library operations provides many benefits. Naturally, there are costs too, but on the whole the balance

Paula Hardin is Digital Project Specialist in the Digital and Preservation Resources Division of OCLC, Dublin, OH. Ms. Hardin has been building large digital libraries for art images with visual resources collections for several years, with experience in the practical implementation issues for taking the analog slide world into the digital realm.

[Haworth co-indexing entry note]: "Integrating the Digitization of Visual Resources into Library Operations." Hardin, Paula. Co-published simultaneously in *Journal of Library Administration* (The Haworth Information Press, an imprint of The Haworth Press, Inc.) Vol. 39, No. 1, 2003, pp. 45-55; and: *The Twenty-First Century Art Librarian* (ed: Terrie L. Wilson) The Haworth Information Press, an imprint of The Haworth Press, Inc., 2003, pp. 45-55. Single or multiple copies of this article are available for a fee from The Haworth Document Delivery Service [1-800-HAWORTH, 9:00 a.m. - 5:00 p.m. (EST). E-mail address: docdelivery@haworthpress.com].

comes out in favor of the benefits. It is useful to know what issues and decisions you need to be aware of for the smooth incorporation of the new technology. *[Article copies available for a fee from The Haworth Document Delivery Service: 1-800-HAWORTH. E-mail address: <docdelivery@haworthpress.com> Website: <http://www.HaworthPress.com> © 2003 by The Haworth Press, Inc. All rights reserved.]*

KEYWORDS. Digitization, visual resources, digitization benefits, digital workflow integration, slide libraries, digital libraries, digitization projects

Access and preservation have been the driving forces behind the development of visual resources digitization projects. When digitization is conceptualized as a *project-based* activity, and access and preservation are the defining goals, process and procedures are established to fit that model. Decisions about a myriad of details cumulate to favor one goal over the other. When access is the primary goal, decisions necessarily emphasize actions to increase the quantity of material digitized. With preservation (meaning the creation of the best possible surrogate) as the main goal, then considerable more procedures and time must be taken to assure the accuracy of the colors, indicators establishing sizes, and other image quality results. In visual resources projects, decisions about the quantity or quality of the images tend to dominate the discussion. However, to optimize access and preservation goals, the data is the unifying component that needs to be as complete and accurate as possible. Addressing the variety of requirements is challenging, especially when there exists the potential dilemma of today's access project turning into tomorrow's preservation project.

When digitization is part of your usual routine, you are able to seize opportunities to exploit that existing base. Integrating digitization into library routine also enhances your capacity to make incremental improvement to images and data as time and opportunity permits. Digitization provides many benefits beyond the goals of access and preservation. Routine digitization of visual resources is a valuable goal in and of itself.

THE DAILY LIFE MODEL FOR DIGITIZATION

Visual resources libraries have traditionally used copy photography from books (and other sources) to make slides for professors and sometimes students. Books are given to the librarian (used generically to mean curator and the many other titles in this role) for processing. Orders of multiple books may exist, or each book might be treated as a single order. Either way, information must be recorded to identify the source as well as data on the person placing the order, the due date (ASAP of course), and enough descriptive data about the object portrayed to create labels for the slides.

Since the digitization process creates image files that need unique names to be saved, the data entry step is best done first so that the unique identifying numbers created during data entry are known for both the slide and the digital images. An automatic serialization field in a database generates the unique accession number. The image file uses that number as the filename with an extension indicating the file type. The digitization of images can take place either before or after the copy photography stage from the books, but would always be done from the books and not the slides.

Museums or other facilities also could integrate digitization into their process by making use of a digital camera for basic documentation of acquisitions. Almost any kind of visual record of all acquisitions would be better than nothing. Of course, it would be beneficial if high quality professional photography of all acquisitions was undertaken as part of the acquisition process, but that is not always possible.

Librarians generally use standard desktop databases to create their own unique implementations of the fields they need to manage their collections. The existing filing schemes of slides and traditional label data have driven the data recorded in the databases. The ad hoc nature of the earlier databases has given way to a concern for standards and many Visual Resources (VR) databases incorporate the Dublin Core or the VRA (Visual Resources Association) Core standards into the database field structures. By following such standards, future interoperability and data sharing will be possible since the appropriate field matches can be made between databases. Core elements evolve in name and other aspects over time, responding to an increased recognition of factors needed to assist sharing of data beyond a narrow focus. For example, the element of "author" would be appropriate for book information but a visual resources equivalent would be "artist" or "architect" rather than "author" as an element name. This divergence is neatly solved by the development of "creator" as an element appropriate for both the book and visual resources data and avoids encouraging the creation of elements for every possible type of creator. The core data elements strive to express the underlying concepts.

The purpose of databases for slides has been the production of slide labels. The integration of digitization procedures into the database operation requires that more attention be given to recording the most complete and accurate data for the object as possible. Building the database as a *finding aid* becomes a major operational goal. Quality controls such as adding "look up tables" to ensure the use of only authorized and consistent terms are needed. The use of authority controls for names, places, and other data helps speed data entry and enhance retrieval by providing limitations of variants. While some databases were built this way in advance of digitization efforts, with digitization as part of daily operations it becomes even more critical to treat data entry very seriously.

PAY AS YOU GO TO SAVE TIME AND MONEY

Everyone has a little pile of slides or other material that just needs one more piece of information or a few details checked. However, the steps needed to retrace the source material, obtain it (if it is still available), fix the database record, and regenerate the slide labels (and let's not forget the backing cards) become time consuming steps put off for one of those "slow" times. It would be ever so nice to incorporate a little research time into the workflow so that certain minimum standards of information could be recorded for each and every acquisition. This necessarily reduces the sheer quantity of new acquisitions possible due to the amount of time involved, but it is possible that at some point the value of complete information will be recognized as worth the trouble it would take to get it. Odds are that "paying" for this research on the spot, incrementally, will cost a lot less than retrospective research. We already have the evidence and experience that tells us that model does not work.

The Source Is with You

If you research now while the book is in your hand it is simply convenient to work with the material and avoid regrets later. It is often tempting to "fill in the blank" even when the source does not specify some information. Sure you may have stood in front of that particular painting and read the card that said it was "oil on canvas" and you may know that with absolute certainty, but do you put that information in the record? If the source in hand does not say it is oil, further research in other sources is necessary. Web searches can be good, but they can also be bad; it depends on the trustworthiness of the site. Memory and guesses are bad ideas to add to a record, so it might be worthwhile to check the bibliography section of the book in hand to find an alternate authoritative source for data.

Basic bibliographic information must be recorded in the database. However, this data is more valuable than just being there for your records. Exploit the resources you have on the data edge, in order to benefit the digitization process. For example, perhaps it would be worthwhile to have a bibliographic reference label on a slide as well. Once placed in the collection, the users might find it valuable to go look for the source for more information or images. Similarly, by printing the acquisition information on the backing cards, even if the slide is circulating, other users could see the information about the book and pursue more information about the item. Since this information would not have to appear at the top of the slide with the filing information, it should fit in some fashion or other. (While not ideal, the identifying number for the record in the database identifying the source would be better than nothing.) With routine scanning of images a part of the acquisition process, thumbnail images might even be printed on backing cards, possibly by printing on the reverse. Being able to see a thumbnail would be very helpful to the users to determine if the slide they are looking for is a particular "untitled" painting.

No Lost Generation Here

When an image is created from an original object, that is a first generation image. When an image is created from the first generation image, that is considered a second-generation image, and so on. Each succeeding generation suffers in quality by being further from the original. Digitization projects using slides for the source of the images suffer a loss of a generation because they are derived from copy photography slides instead of being digitized directly from the pictures in a book. And of course, the images in the books were likely created from photographs or slides from a derivative of an original transformed into a digital image suitable for printing, and so forth.

In VR operations, digitization is often conceptualized as scanning from newly created transparencies, even though that may mean they would be scanned after they are mounted under glass. The glass layer is needed to protect the slides when they circulate, but scanning through the glass to create a digital image adds another impeding layer to the process.

By creating the digital images directly from the books as part of the acquisition process, there is no loss of generation to the slide intermediary. Of course, the slide is still created as the usual step in the operation, at least for now, though the day may come when that step is no longer needed. The benefits of scanning directly from the books instead of slide derivatives are even more apparent with large images. Direct scanning allows the capture of detail at a much higher level than is possible when copy photography of a full-page image reduces it to fit on a 35mm slide. Too much detail gets lost trying to capture large items, especially those not of slide proportions (such as double page images). You could shoot details, but it is difficult to predict what someone might find to be a useful detail. To acquire large images it is helpful to use a "tabloid" size (11″ × 17″) scanner. The usual flatbed scanner size is 8 1/2 × 14 inches, the size of a sheet of legal paper. With large books, trying to fit a single side of the books onto the bed becomes an exercise in weight lifting combined with minuscule adjustments left-to-right or top-to-bottom to fit the whole image on in one scanner pass. This is hard on the staff, the books, and time consuming to make and check the completeness of the preview images. With the larger, 11″ × 17″ size flatbed scanners, most large books will fit without too many props or muscles holding them in place. Larger beds are better for items like maps too, since obtaining the most coverage possible in one "pass" of the scanner will reduce the need to "stitch" those partial images together using PhotoShop or some other image manipulation software.

Flatbed Scanning and Seeing Dots

Images in books are printed using patterns of dots. Color printing consists of combinations of colored dots (cyan, magenta, yellow, and black) all printed so they do not overprint each other, but appear side by side. The arrangement of dots can cause the resulting scan to have strange patterns and look very spotty. These are moire patterns and they do not tend to show up as distinctly on slides. This does not mean the scans are better off being made from slides rather than directly from book pages, but there are techniques you should use to mitigate the problem. The first trick is to pay attention to the direction you place the book on the flatbed. If the scan shows odd color patterns, try shifting the book to another orientation (try horizontal if the original scanning direction was vertical, for example). Sometimes even a diagonal direction will help reduce the problem.

Another technique to reduce problems when scanning from printed images is to use a "descreening" feature often found with scanner software. The "screening" that is being corrected is the dot pattern that results from the shifting of the colors during printing. If this feature is not available at the time of scanning, PhotoShop's Gaussian Blur can be used to blur the image in a way that reduces the screen patterns. With the "preview" option selected, it is easy to make incremental adjustments and see how far to push the process. (Blur features in PhotoShop are found in the Filter menu.) The use of the Gaussian Blur is followed by the use of another filter, the Unsharp Mask filter, to sharpen the image. Because they operate on the image differently, the use of the Unsharp Mask filter will not simply return the image to the previous moire state (although some pattern traces may remain in some images).

In addition to being able to redo scans several times as needed with the book in hand, it is also possible to match colors to the images in the books, which hopefully have been checked with original objects or other information. It is possible to go into a production mode and just scan a bunch of images and plan to use PhotoShop later, but that is probably not a real time savings since it takes only a few minutes for an experienced person to tidy up images on the spot. To identify a particular file name to fix later or entire folders with items to be adjusted can be confusing and may result in raw scans being added to the digital collection without realizing it. This would throw the process back to the "little piles of slides" stage, retrospectively determining what the proper rotation, colors, and so forth should be for scans with no source available.

THE IMAGE IS METADATA

It is difficult to tell which "untitled" painting an image is from cataloging information. Likewise it is hard to determine which view of an "East Portal" or which self-portrait of the many Rembrandt did is described by simple text. The actual image is required to determine if it is the one you are seeking. This means that the image itself is data about data: metadata.

The visual statement of images is not fully expressed in simple text fields. A description or similar section might help (for example, "holding a book") to convey particular distinguishing details. But only seeing an image provides the certainty that it is the right image. For collections of images, therefore, it is vital and necessary to record the images themselves so that the image as metadata component is treated as a data element.

It is not usually advisable to include images in database records, even as thumbnail sizes (125 to 150 pixels maximum generally). The databases are capable of containing them, but tend to be slowed down in providing retrieval results due to the additional processing time required. Other software manages to do this better, and these are the image management packages, or "imagebases" if a parallel term becomes accepted.

The image is so valuable as metadata for visual resource collections that it would be worthwhile to retrospectively scan all of the slides in a library to capture the full and accurate picture of the library holdings. For this purpose, the complete inventory of the holdings, even slides in the worst condition should be scanned. I could go on for pages as to why this should be done, but that is not what this article is about. In a nutshell, it is most efficient and effective to scan everything. Get all the data entry done. Use this information, including looking for unfixed "pink" images if you wish (though that means you have to be sure *not* to fix them in PhotoShop) to make decisions about the collection. Then de-accessioning, replacements, and other collections maintenance issues can be based on firm data and not on what may or may not be in the collection in a usable condition. Someone might even question the scanning of "duplicate" images. I would argue that if they have an accession number, they are part of the collection, and that an accurate database and imagebase of the collection must show the duplicates (and these would have unique accession numbers despite the content being, potentially, duplicate). Without such information on duplicates, how can you do an analysis to decide what may or may not warrant duplication, such as may be needed for pivotal works in high demand? I would also argue that if a "pink" slide is not worth scanning, then it is not worth having in the slide collection either, and yet I would wager than very few librarians would go through their collection and deaccession a slide because it was pink.

With batch feeders, hundreds of scans could be created on a daily basis. It takes time though to process them in PhotoShop while the slides are still in hand, and longer still to retrospectively add records. This makes it difficult to incorporate retrospective scanning and data entry in daily operations. One possible way to do so is to make digitization a part of the circulation process. When slides are returned, scan them. This has the advantage of building in a check for verifying that a particular item was returned. It also leverages the value of the digital collection because it is built on items known to be in demand.

Of course, nothing is ever that simple. Once routine acquisition scanning is incorporated into operations, it can become tricky to add retrospective scanning into the mix. You must make sure than all new acquisition slides are identified as having been scanned before they are filed for circulation. If you do not clearly mark the slides, a process to retrospectively scan slides will result in the creation of digital images from the *slides* that actually already have better digital images online. Both scans would be assigned the same name, but depending on the file management process, you might end up with one or both scans, and confusion abounding. This mistaken duplication of scans would also be a waste of resources. The simple act of writing an "S" for scanned on the slide can save this from happening. Even new acquisitions need this note, plus a "D" for data entered, otherwise once slides from mixed processing start coming through, it is difficult to determine their status and requirements. In fact, it is probably a good idea to include a "P" for PhotoShop since that is a distinct stage that would not take place when slides are batch scanned. Then too, it is good to be consistent in the placement of the letters on the slides since you will become accustomed to quickly scanning the slides for these codes, prior to loading circulated items into a batch feeder. Of course you must also make some kind of notation in the database records for items that have been digitized for all kinds of reporting purposes, including potential statistics about the digital collection for possible grants. Perhaps in the not so distant future you will also need to identify which items in your collection are "digital only" images with no slides of them at all.

DIGITAL COLLECTIONS MEANS MANAGING MULTIPLE LIBRARIES

There are benefits in making digitization a routine part of operations. It can foster the improvement of data quality and completeness thereby increasing both access and retrieval. The image is an essential piece of data as equal if not more so than the textual description that is only captured in the digitization process. When making an effort to find a set of slides, it is very helpful to be able to call up a view of the items online for perfect identification of the images that belong to an order. If you have 10 scans and only 9 slides, it is immediately obvious that something is wrong with an order. If it is difficult to tell the proper orientation of an abstract painting while mounting the slide after the reserve book it came from has been returned, a quick check of the scan will show the right direction. Crosschecking slides to printouts of thumbnails can also indicate possible "flipped" slides that are mounted backwards. All of these precautions result in better quality slides and order processing.

Just examining the creation and use of the digital images in lieu of slides is another way of evaluating the value of digitization. By not making slides, the significant costs associated with the purchase of film, processing, mounts, labels, and labor to perform these tasks is eliminated. In a time of tight budgets, when the technical infrastructure is mandated or in place already for digital display, it becomes more difficult to justify thousands of dollars being spent on slides that often are not used more than once for a class. For people in a hurry, eliminating the labor-intensive process of slide creation in favor of the digital image should be a tremendous attraction. With flatbed scanners cheap and the books in hand, professors could experience instant gratification and show material without caring about the data since they would provide that in their lectures. (Mind you I am not advocating this as a desirable thing, merely establishing that if speed is the priority, digital can meet that need far better than slides.)

The physicality of slides limits the display to the number permitted by slide carousels. The standard slide carousel has 80 slots (the larger quantity carousels are not often used as the slots are much thinner and glass mounted slides tend to jam), and most often two carousels are used to compare and contrast images. Obviously, the dual projection limits the display to two images, and people have become accustomed to thinking about material presentation in this manner only. With digital, a classroom presentation is not limited to the number of slides that can fit in two carousels. Any desired image from an entire semester's lectures could be retrieved as quickly as the technical savvy of the professor allows. The time it takes to pull and place the slides in the carousels for lectures is eliminated for professors, and the refiling time for visual resources librarians is eliminated as well. Imagine the overall benefits of reallocating 20 hours (or more!) to tasks other than filing, including doing more (digital of course) acquisition or collection management work. One of the most common uses of digital images from visual resources collections is to provide web pages of images for student review of material covered in classes. In other words, the images are being created and used online in some fashion, but slides are still being created and pulled and filed and so on in the visual resources library. So despite the numerous and real benefits of going digital, visual resources libraries remain what they have been for years: slide libraries.

What this means is that with any portion of digitization added to slide library operations, you are also faced with organizing, maintaining, and protecting the digital masters as well as the slides themselves. It is a lot trickier to manage non-physical objects, especially since it takes but a moment to delete the digital assets by the thousands, or to accidentally wipe out all the web display size images with the batch process used to create thumbnails. Duplicate and other numbering problems abound. Version control is a constant issue. At various stages of development there seem to be points at which you hit "walls" of difficulty, for example, at 7,000 images for no known reason, things just become more complicated. It suddenly becomes harder to keep track of all the stages, fixes, and other requirements of the digital objects. Whether digitization is project-based or routine operations-based, more work is still more work.

CONCLUSION

Some direct benefit to the library and library staff is realized by leveraging digitization where possible to help manage traditional slide library operations. Incorporating digitization into the acquisition process will distribute and reduce the future workload of retrospective conversion (which we all know is coming). Circulation management can be improved while preparing the library for future retrospective conversion by digitizing circulated slides. Digital libraries are the future for visual resources, so it is a good idea to start thinking of the digitization process as far more than a project or a temporary supplemental activity. Incorporate digitization into routine operations now and become prepared for that future.

Management, Public Service, and Access Issues: Serving Special Collections in an Architecture Branch Library

Janine Jacqueline Henri

SUMMARY. Administering special collections within an academic branch library presents challenges in the areas of public services, collection management, facilities planning, and staffing. In art and architecture libraries, special collections can include a variety of materials such as rare books, trade catalogs, builder's guides, graphic and visual materials, artists' books, archival records in many formats, and files of ephemera. Public service issues relating to the administration of special collections housed in an architecture branch library (and its off-site repositories) will be addressed. Collection care and access services will be examined in light of recent technologies. *[Article copies available for a fee from The Haworth Document Delivery Service: 1-800-HAWORTH. E-mail address: <docdelivery@haworthpress.com> Website: <http://www.HaworthPress.com> © 2003 by The Haworth Press, Inc. All rights reserved.]*

KEYWORDS. Special collections, architecture libraries, art librarianship, branch libraries

Janine Jacqueline Henri is Head Librarian, Architecture and Planning Library, The General Libraries, P.O. Box P, The University of Texas at Austin, Austin, TX 78713-8916 (E-mail: jhenri@mail.utexas.edu).

[Haworth co-indexing entry note]: "Management, Public Service, and Access Issues: Serving Special Collections in an Architecture Branch Library." Henri, Janine Jacqueline. Co-published simultaneously in *Journal of Library Administration* (The Haworth Information Press, an imprint of The Haworth Press, Inc.) Vol. 39, No. 1, 2003, pp. 57-76; and: *The Twenty-First Century Art Librarian* (ed: Terrie L. Wilson) The Haworth Information Press, an imprint of The Haworth Press, Inc., 2003, pp. 57-76. Single or multiple copies of this article are available for a fee from The Haworth Document Delivery Service [1-800-HAWORTH, 9:00 a.m. - 5:00 p.m. (EST). E-mail address: docdelivery@haworthpress.com].

10.1300/J111v39n01_04

SPECIAL COLLECTION MATERIAL TYPES
IN ART AND ARCHITECTURE LIBRARIES

Many academic art and architecture branch libraries in North America include special collections among their holdings. These collections can include rare books and periodicals, architectural treatises, artists' books, portfolios of loose plates, materials needing protection due to fragile condition, unusual format, the presence of original prints, or potential high replacement costs, as well as graphic and photographic materials, files of ephemera, trade catalogs, builder's guides, works of art, audio-visual materials, architectural drawings, models, manufacturer's samples, and archival records in a variety of formats.[1] "Special collections contain material that are unique to the library: . . . Reasons put forth for keeping these collections in closed stacks include rarity, physical condition, unprocessed/uncataloged status, and limited staffing. Most special collections are housed at separate locations or in spaces too small for browsing."[2] Some art and architecture libraries even specify in their collection development policies what types of materials they collect.[3]

In their article "Snow Globes, Valentines, Mail Art, Oh My!: Weird and Wonderful Art Library Collections," Jane Carlin and Adrienne Varady describe some of the unusual formats found in art and architecture libraries.[4] Gallery invitations, greeting cards, games, toys, scrapbooks, and even snow globes are housed in art library collections. These items "offer the patron and researcher a unique view into our cultural heritage, and can serve as an important primary resource for scholars. These 'weird and wonderful' curiosities engage the user and serve as a way to publicize and exploit the services and resources of the library."[5] Many material types are collected by art libraries as documents or evidence of specific forms or genres. In addition to their research value, Carlin and Varady contend that "unusual collections can be major assets in fund-raising and public outreach."[6] According to Clive Phillpot, "It is a truism that researchers will travel the greatest distances to see the smallest fragments of information or to visit obscure collections of document files (as well as archival collections), the reason being that these collections have the most singularity of all the components of an art library and are not duplicable in other locations."[7] Although this statement is perhaps less true now that researchers expect more and more document-delivery to their desktops, it still serves to illustrate the importance of collections of unique, unusual, or obscure material.

Typically special collection materials are housed in a separate closed stacks area of the branch library, while the rest of the collection is open for browsing. Because of their prevalence in art and architecture libraries, the Art Libraries Society of North America (ARLIS/NA) includes collections of special materials in their *Facilities Standards for Art Libraries and Visual Resource Collections.*[8] In 1985 ARLIS/NA surveyed art libraries[9] and 136 responded (an 86% response rate). Of these, 61% reported open stacks access except for special collections and another 37% reported open stacks access except for 'other' (which included artists' books, reserves, and non-book formats). As far as materials collected, 38% reported collecting photographs, 26% art reproductions, 36% picture files, 3% vertical files, 12.5% original art, while 40% reported collecting 'other' such as architectural drawings, archives, artists' books, book jackets, manuscripts, maps, postcards, scrapbooks, trade literature, and audio-visual materials.[10] (A follow-up survey would be of interest: Has the situation changed dramatically since 1985?) Clearly a common feature of art and architecture libraries has been that they house a variety of material types.

Out of a mean total facility area of 7,575 square feet, libraries responding to the 1985 survey dedicated 511 square feet to special/rare collections (almost 15% of their total space). Another 298 square feet was dedicated to 'other areas' that included archives storage, multipurpose rooms, seminar, listening, and video viewing rooms.[11] Indeed, in addition to storage space, libraries with special collections must also allocate space for viewing these materials. To justify being collected, housed, and serviced by our libraries, one must assume that these special materials are in demand by our clientele.

GUIDELINES FOR ACADEMIC BRANCH LIBRARIES

Academic branch libraries are usually designed to support the information and research needs of specific departments, colleges, schools, or disciplines. Services and collecting policies are tailored to the specific needs of the branch's primary user group. According to the "ACRL Guidelines for Branch Libraries in Colleges and Universities," the "primary mission of the branch library is to provide information and access to information to meet the instructional and research needs of its user group. A branch library's programs must provide for the requirements of its primary clientele as well as the cross-disciplinary needs of others in the academic community."[12] In addition, the guidelines state that the "value of a collection is determined by its usability as well as by its quality and size. . . . the collections must be adequately housed with

proper environmental controls and systematically arranged in an under-
standable fashion, with safeguards against loss, mutilation, and theft, so
that they are accessible to all users."[13] According to Mary Ellen Dusey,
"The highest priorities for an archive or a special collection remain security, long-time protection of materials, and access."[14] To safeguard
against loss or damage due to improper handling, the special collection
stacks at the University of Texas' Architecture and Planning Library are
only accessible to the librarian, the Circulation Services Supervisor,
and the Night/Week-End Supervisors. Of course, the environmental
conditions in which we store our materials are an important factor in
their preservation. The preservation and conservation section of the
branch guidelines asks us to consider moving rare or fragile materials to
a more protected environment if conditions within the branch are not
adequate.[15] General criteria for proper environmental conditions in
which to house material types commonly found in art and architecture
collections are outlined by Susan Swartzburg in her "Preservation Considerations in Developing Library Space."[16] Carolee Griffin has also
succinctly reviewed some of the major conservation and preservation
treatment issues faced by fine arts libraries.[17] In addition, part of our ob-
ligation to our collections entails appropriate disaster planning.
ARLIS/NL (The Netherlands) recently drafted guidelines for disaster
planning by art libraries. A list of essential issues to consider when preparing disaster plans together with a handy bibliography is also available from the National Library of Australia.[18]

In his article "The Continuing Debate over Academic Branch Libraries," Leo Shkolnik mentions that "immediate accessibility is the
most important feature in the use of books."[19] But he believes that the
arguments about centralization and decentralization may have been rendered moot by new technologies: Where the information is located is no
longer important, it is how quickly the patron receives it that matters.
Similarly, Olivia Madison, Sally Frey, and David Gregory contend that
"new technologies will undoubtedly play a pivotal role in determining
the optimal physical organization of future library systems."[20] Charlotte Crockett, in her discussion of branch libraries states that traditionally "university libraries have favored the centralized model, but
teaching faculty have preferred branch libraries, with their strong ties
and services to individual departments."[21] Although she believes that
"we can look at the possibility of centralized book collections (largely
in off-campus storage) but decentralized subject expertise and access to
information, all rendered effective through newer means of storage and
communication," I would argue that this model does not work well for

users and collections where browsing is an important mode of retrieving information.[22] Our Library of Congress subject headings are of no use when the user is looking for illustrations that show a particular color of wall treatment adjacent to a variety of textures and materials! (Which books or periodical articles would we retrieve from storage for this user?) I firmly believe that art and architecture branch libraries with print collections will continue to be necessary on most academic campuses until the ability to visually browse the contents of our collections can be replicated from our user's desktops.

PHYSICAL AND INTELLECTUAL ACCESS ISSUES

When a significant portion of our collections' use is a result of students browsing the stacks (looking for design precedents, examples of recent work, or just for inspiration without any specific subject in mind), how does one facilitate the use of closed stacks material? For those with adequate resources to support such an endeavor, illustrated guides to special collection holdings are an excellent means of outreach. A fine example of such a tool is the *Library of Congress Prints and Photographs: An Illustrated Guide* (available both in print and online versions).[23] Even a more modest publication, represented in our catalogs, linked on our web sites, and retrievable through appropriate web searches, should help researchers discover our hidden resources.[24]

Faced with a substantial special collection partly shelved on a locked floor (not visible to users) and partly shelved off campus, I found myself wanting to publicize its existence and promote its use. The books and periodicals housed in the University of Texas at Austin's Architecture and Planning Library Special Collections are all represented in our online catalog. Some of the catalog records even include searchable provenance notes.[25] Searchers willing to use the catalog can easily discover these materials. Our online catalog also includes a collection-level record for the *Texas Architecture Archive*, a growing collection of files housed in our special collection stacks that document individual buildings in Texas with reports, photographs, oral histories, videos, drawings, and other records produced by School of Architecture students as part of coursework. Card file access has been maintained for each report (arranged by county, city, then building name or address). This information has now been entered in a database that we hope to make web accessible.[26] Users must request special collection items from our Circulation Desk, and a desk supervisor or the librarian pages the material which is checked out for two-hour use in the library, and must be used at a specially designated table adjacent to the Circulation Desk (so that use can be monitored). Every effort is made to insure that appropriate staff is available every hour that the library is open to facilitate special collection access.[27] No pens are allowed on the Special Collections table and book pillows are provided when warranted (gloves are also provided when handling materials with metal clasps, gilding, or with original photographs).[28] Because photocopying of special collection items by users is not usually permitted, a room with a camera stand is made available for those wishing to photograph materials. However, this does not usually serve the needs of those desiring publication-quality prints. For these individuals we make arrangements for reproductions through the university's photographic services department. For the special collection materials that are shelved off site at the Charles W. Moore Center for the Study of Place, the same rules apply, but users must fill out a hold card just as they would for a regular collection item shelved in our library storage facility. Every effort is made to page items within a reasonable turn around time, but we do not have a regular shuttle service to the Center (as we do to the storage facility), and we must make appointments to visit the Center in order to retrieve our materials.[29]

One way that I have publicized our special collections is by giving 'behind the scenes' tours to new faculty members or to small groups of students in conjunction with a library orientation session. Faculty and students are walked through the closed stacks to enable them to visualize the size of the collections and to note the variety of formats present, from miniature books to elephant folios and files of ephemera.[30] I usually pull out examples that I believe might be of special interest to the faculty or students, and I explain the access procedures as well as restrictions on use. Also, I have selected material for display in the library during orientations, open houses, and bibliographic instruction sessions, mounted exhibits in locked display cases, prepared press releases to announce new major acquisitions, [31] and have even taken material to classrooms for viewing. Although we do not have a group study room in the Architecture and Planning Library, there is a seminar room in the building that I have been able to reserve when a faculty member has asked about showing specific items to their classes. Students in architecture history courses have examined early builder's guides this way, and folios of nineteenth century plates of landscape views have been shown to students in an art history course dealing with the picturesque. At least once a year for the last few years I have taken Josef Albers' *In-*

teraction of Color[32] to a class of interior design students that meets in another building on campus. Of course, during each classroom presentation I can say a few words about our special collections and how to access them. Besides promoting the use of special collection materials, these services to classes have also facilitated more cooperation between library staff and faculty and have resulted in an increase in librarian consultations by students from these classes. As a result of these interactions I believe that once students are aware of the extent and potential usefulness of our special collections, they are more willing to learn the subject searching intricacies needed to locate relevant records in our catalog. Other branch libraries where special collections are visible behind locked glass-fronted cabinets may not need to resort to tours through closed stacks to achieve the same result: Users can see the materials in the locked cases, and they are able to perform at least a cursory form of browsing.

Antoinette Nelson and Pollyanne Frantz contend that "librarians who work with closed collections must analyze their user's information needs and develop philosophies and strategies for meeting them."[33] Collection security concerns need to be balanced with users' information needs. Staffing, budgeting, planning, as well as circulation, reference, and cataloging functions should facilitate the provision of information resources to today's users while preserving collections for future uses. The following keys to access are identified: "card catalogs, online catalogs, subject bibliographies, vertical file indexes, newsletters, stack card privileges for serious researchers, new-material display cases, and pathfinders (finding aids)."[34] One example of a solution for improving intellectual access to ephemeral material in an art library (by creating a cataloging template for artists files and other records) is discussed by Daniel Starr in "Cataloging Artist Files: One Library's Approach to Providing Integrated Access to Ephemeral Material."[35] Additional examples of enhanced access through cataloging include adding provenance notes, copy specific notes, and form and genre terms. The latter terms are crucial for our users' ability to retrieve examples of graphic materials. Of course their usefulness is limited by the catalog's (and the user's) ability to search and retrieve this information. Other approaches include creating special bibliographies (lists of typography materials for instance, since the subjects of books collected as examples of a typographer's work often have no relevance to the retrieval needs of graphic arts students) or creating pathfinders (finding aids) for specific collections of material. Like many other archival repositories, the Alexander Architectural Archive at the University of

Texas at Austin is participating in a cooperative project to convert finding aids to EAD/DTD format and place them in a searchable web site.[36] The archival finding aid model is an excellent solution for improving intellectual access to materials that cannot receive item-level cataloging. Of course, our ability to undertake these activities depends on available staffing.

Special collections are mentioned in the "ACRL Guidelines for the Preparation of Policies on Library Access."[37] Considerations listed in the guidelines include: security issues, policies on duplication (including user fees, etc.), and interlibrary loan policies. Megan Mulder mentions that digital imaging and full-text databases have emerged as new means to provide access to special collections materials.[38] She points to the University of Virginia's Electronic Text Center as a good example of a site that provides access to documents that were often previously only available in a limited number of copies.[39] With many web links to electronic versions of texts included in catalog records located in international databases such as OCLC and RLIN (and an increasing volume of interlibrary loan requests being delivered electronically), users now expect to access more and more unique resources from their desktops. But as Mulder says, ". . . there is not a practical alternative to every interlibrary loan request. Many items are too large or too fragile for photocopying or photographing."[40] This is especially true for architecture materials where bound elephant folios are not uncommon. She quotes the "Draft Guidelines for the Loan of Rare and Unique Materials" as stating: "Refusals either to lend or copy a requested item should include a specific reason (e.g., fragile paper, tight binding, too large to ship safely, etc.). That an item is part of a special collection is not sufficient reason."[41] But Connell Gallagher believes that both archivists and special collection librarians need policies for lending materials. He expects more requests for these materials as more collections are described in network accessible databases. Indeed, collections are built and preserved with the expectation that they will be used.[42] Unfortunately, due to the lack of appropriate photocopying equipment (and the high cost of copiers with book cradles that accommodate oversized materials), I find myself turning away more and more interlibrary loan requests just as my collection of rare or scarce materials is growing.

The Library of Congress has recently implemented an innovative pilot project to explore the possibility of digitizing public domain material requested through interlibrary loan.[43] Once scanned, a link is provided from the bibliographic record to the digital file. The reasoning here is that if an item is requested once, it might well be needed again, and once digitized they can reduce the item's future handling. For those of us with unique or scarce materials, this is an option worth investigating. Of course, access to proper equipment and proper handling procedures for fragile materials must be worked out before such projects are undertaken. If we consider that we provide fee-based photographic duplication services for our archival materials, would not digital reproductions be an extension of this service? Some repositories such as the Special Collections at Louisiana State University are indeed already doing this.[44] If we are concerned about the cost of equipment and staffing for this service, why not outsource it to trusted professionals as some of us already do for the reproduction of our architectural drawings? Another model for digitization on demand is the model currently used for electronic reserves. If we can identify special collection items that get repeated use as part of course assignments, perhaps these would be good candidates for digitization. (If these materials are in the public domain we would not need to restrict access to their digital copies as we currently do with most electronic reserves.)

David Cobb mentions that "Improving access to materials should be one of the goals for all librarians and libraries."[45] He maintains that contrary to the belief that the digital age will open access to all materials, digital access also results in increasing limits to access. In the context of a map collection he sees the following limits: hours, and the resultant limit to access to professional reference service; the fragile nature of maps and their poor condition due to the ravages of time, environment, and handling; the level of cataloging (including the lack of analytics) and the percentage of uncataloged material; copyright and other intellectual property rights; limits caused by permission fees. Certainly these limits are also present in art and architecture collections. Reducing cataloging backlogs and improving cataloging levels are goals that might be accomplished with appropriate support from the central administration and by reallocating priorities and staff. Cobb points out that most research libraries provide special collection photo-reproduction services. He suspects that some libraries charge more than they have to for these services, to restrict them so that the volume of requests does not overwhelm their limited staff. He is concerned that researching and selecting materials for imaging requests received via email, regular mail, and telephone might take staff away from other primary duties. He sees the future bringing more customized services, and believes that while libraries will expand their offerings through the web, nominal fees will need to be charged to offset customized reference services.[46] Indeed, at the University of Texas at Austin we add a handling fee and a preservation fee to our charges for reproductions, in order to recover part of the labor costs associated with these services. However, we consider our reference service activities primary duties and have not sought to limit them by imposing fees.

PUBLIC RELATIONS ISSUES

According to Leslie Morris, "Exhibitions of rare books and manuscripts are increasingly seen as an important medium through which curators can make special collections more accessible to both the scholarly and nonspecialist public."[47] But the installation is only one way to "communicate through an exhibition." Publications and exhibition programming are alternate approaches that can be good public relations tools. They also provide opportunities to go beyond the materials in the exhibition cases. She suggests organizing exhibitions in conjunction with an event planned by someone else, as a 'tie-in' to guarantee at least a minimum audience. In an academic branch library, obvious tie-ins could be classes and seminars, guest lectures in the departments we support, or other campus events. At the Southeastern Architectural Archive[48] at Tulane University, students regularly research and prepare exhibitions featuring archival and special collections as part of their coursework. The University of Brighton has held student book arts competitions and exhibitions, accompanied by talks given by practitioners and art critics. Among the incentives to participate: The library purchases some student pieces for its artists' books collection![49] Relations with faculty might be facilitated through exhibits highlighting new acquisitions of particular interest to them and donor relations can often be promoted when exhibiting new donations or current collections that relate to a potential donor's interests.[50] ANSI/NISO standards for environmental conditions for exhibiting library and archival materials are available to guide us when preparing exhibits.[51] In addition, the Rare Book and Manuscripts Section of the American Library Association has published guidelines for borrowing special collection materials for exhibitions.[52]

Any exhibition requires selection of material, often around a theme or highlighting a particular aspect of the collection. Once this material is selected for exhibit, why not consider an accompanying virtual exhibit as well? This does not necessarily entail digitizing entire publications, though with proper copyright permission, this might be a way to expand the exhibit beyond what can be displayed in a case. This approach serves both as a public relations tool, to advertise the contents of special collections, and as a 'permanent' documentation of the exhibit, much as a print exhibition catalog would.[53] Of course, we can also create virtual exhibits that do not have print counterparts: A distinct advantage of digital exhibits is that they can be left online indefinitely as they do not expose artifacts to harmful elements such as light.[54]

DIGITIZATION ISSUES

Recent literature about special collections shows a marked trend towards taking advantage of digitization technologies to increase virtual access to special collection materials.[55] This has several advantages: fewer paging requests (and resultant reshelving) mean that library staff is available for other projects. Fewer requests for viewing originals will also result in less wear on them and should aid in their preservation. However, the digitization process does require substantial handling and staff time as well as access to proper equipment and an ongoing commitment to maintain digital files. Equipment is a special problem for art and architecture collections that often contain oversize bound materials and photosensitive media. Peter Hirtle outlines the perceived benefits of digitization.[56] One such benefit is increased use of collections: Material that might have seemed obscure in hard copy can become a core resource once digitized and widely available. New types of research as well as new users and new uses have also been reported as benefits. For instance, some scanned images have revealed text that could not otherwise be seen, and K-12 users are now consulting the digital surrogates of rare books and manuscripts normally restricted to scholars. These benefits are seen by libraries across the country as justifications to undertake digitization projects. To these justifications I would add donor relations: Digitizing collections to make them more widely available is a topic that donors have brought up more and more frequently during gift negotiations. To be able to continue to attract the donor base we covet, we may well need to demonstrate that our libraries are committed to the provision of digital access to our unique resources.

Hirtle believes that despite the poor ergonomics of many electronic display systems, most use of paper copies will be replaced by electronic access. He notes that digital facsimiles overcome physical access issues such as a library's limited hours and concludes that readers only interested in texts will prefer digital copies. Of course this will not be so when the physical nature of the artifact is the primary motivation for us-

ing the material, as can be the case with many art and design materials!
With only anecdotal evidence and the belief that the surrogate is more
convenient, he foresees the use of paper originals decreasing and the
number of books available as digital facsimiles increasing. He predicts
that in thirty years most of the volumes in library print special collections will be available online as digital surrogates. "Special collections
print holdings will become less special."[57] He even questions the need
for libraries to keep all of their copies of print titles (or to purchase print
copies) once surrogates are available online. Again this is applicable
only if the copy is collected for its text's informational value rather than
for its value as an artifact. However, selective deaccessioning certainly
would be a viable alternative to numerous branch libraries individually
caring for brittle copies of items that are not unique artifacts. Hirtle believes that special collections librarianship will change, and he wonders
who will answer the reference questions relating to digitized special
materials: general reference librarians rather than specialists? Art and
architecture branch librarians might not have special rare book training,
but they do have subject expertise and collection-specific knowledge
that is valued by their users and colleagues. My personal belief is that
we will continue to network with each other so that we can continue to
make appropriate referrals.

Peter Hirtle's vision for the future of special collections is that collections will need to emphasize those elements in their holdings that are
truly unique. Indeed, just as preservation microfilming projects entail
searching for records of previous microfilming projects so as not to duplicate efforts, digitization projects involving special collections materials should do likewise. Only when marginalia or other special features
distinguish the originals should we consider digitizing another copy. Instead Hirtle urges us to improve special collection access tools. In addition, he believes that "we can reinvigorate the idea of special collections
as museums"[58] because of the artifactual value of our materials. In the
future, he wants us to "stress the artifactual value of the works more,
both in collecting material and in presenting it to users. Online surrogates will be able to deliver the content of books; we need to identify
and stress the value of books as objects in the special collections museum of the future. It also means that in collection development the emphasis should be on acquiring books that are meaningful as artifacts and
not just rare or expensive."[59]

Most art librarians are well attuned to issues of provenance, as they
are often called upon to assist users with provenance research questions.
In architecture collections with archival holdings (such as at the Univer-

sity of Texas at Austin), entire libraries of architects or firms are often acquired in conjunction with archival collections. This practice enables researchers to compare an architect's built work with the precedents illustrated in that architect's library.[60] Some architects sketch in their books and these marginalia enlighten scholars to the development of design ideas. Other architects have taken publications apart, gathered material together by building type or design elements, and rebound them or created scrapbooks. These collections become evidence of professional practice methods. Peter Graham notes that many rare book and manuscript collections now include digitization projects as part of their activities and he believes that the skills of rare book librarians and curators will continue to be essential in the networked environment. He contends that "readers come to the library to find information in books and, less often (though importantly), to study the book as object to gain further information about the text or about history more broadly considered."[61] Of course, collections of artists' books, books with moveable parts (such as pop-up books) and realia are obvious exceptions that are indeed studied as objects by art and design students or scholars. Design students often find that there is no substitute for seeing and handling the original artifact. They often want to feel the weight and texture of the paper and binding (and sometimes even want to smell the ink!). Other print materials not well suited to digitization include titles where the reflected nature of light on paper is an important part of what is communicated by an illustration. (The CD-ROM version of Josef Albers' *Interaction of Color* is an example where art and architecture library users found that the nature of refracted light from video display terminals prevents full understanding of the exercises.)[62] Graham points out that electronic collections are not special and there is no need to protect them against use. "Use will not damage an electronic work."[63] For art librarians this is an important point: Some items are placed in our special collections for protection, not only because of their fragility or rarity, but because of their high potential for mutilation or theft. When copyright issues can be resolved for these materials, expanded access through digital facsimile should be a boon to our users.

Now that RLG and OCLC have issued their *Final Report on Trusted Digital Repositories: Attributes and Responsibilities*,[64] I anticipate less reluctance to consider digitization to provide access to items that cannot receive repeated handling. (The reluctance has often been over the lack of longevity of digital files.) With the maturation of standards, digital reformatting for preservation purposes can now be considered seriously. The University of Edinburgh has recently announced online access to

Charting the Nation, a collection of historic maps of Scotland and related texts that were digitized because they are fragile, unique, or rare, and to aid in their long term conservation (as well as to bring related materials from several collections together and make them accessible in an innovative way).[65] The benefits are increased access and reduced handling of originals. For researchers, and reference librarians alike, the ability to virtually collocate related materials that are spread out across several repositories is a major advantage of the web. Another cooperative endeavor that intends to result in this kind of improved access is the *Greene and Greene Virtual Archives Project* undertaken by the University of California at Berkeley's Environmental Design Archives, the Avery Library at Columbia, and the University of Southern California (Gamble House) with the Huntington Library.[66]

Setting preservation concerns aside, according to Jennifer Durran, the "needs of the core activities of the discipline–scholarship and research–should be the prime focus of imaging projects as opposed to the needs of the organization."[67] Digitization projects of special interest to our branch library constituents could be a result of faculty research interests, or they might highlight unique resources that have regional or statewide significance. An example of a resource that supports disciplinary research needs is the University of Wisconsin Madison's *Digital Library for the Decorative Arts and Material Culture*.[68] Model projects that highlight collections of statewide interest are Texas A&M's *Images of a Rural Past*[69] and the pioneering efforts of the Louisiana State University Libraries' Electronic Imaging Laboratory.[70] In addition, just as some unique material in art and architecture collections has been reproduced in facsimile form or microfilmed to enable distribution to other collections (think of the trade catalog and artist's file collections for instance),[71] some of our holdings might well be of interest to publishers of digital collections. One model for such a project is the *Gerritsen Collection: Women's History Online, 1543-1945*.[72] Obviously this scenario is most appropriate for collections of unique material that have broad (commercial) appeal.

CONCLUSION

Simon Ford warns us that those texts "that are not accessible through the new media, as they achieve cultural dominance, will become marginalized, insignificant, and practically nonexistent."[73] Managers of unique collections therefore have an important role to play in insuring access to their holdings. According to Graham:

Placing digitized materials on the network already has become a requirement for present day special collections departments. Rare book departments and treasure collections always have played a role in enhancing the prestige of their institutions. Many university administrators (and some librarians) already have seized on the public relations potential of placing digitized versions of attractive holdings on the network; . . . In the long run, when consistently organized and funded, digitizing projects will prove of real value for libraries and their users–and for many materials.[74]

As with all projects, costs need to be weighed against benefits. Selecting material for digitization can be a challenge unless a project is well conceived. There are many models of digitization projects in use by special collections that can be adopted by art and architecture libraries. Academic branch librarians are well positioned to know the needs of their users, and therefore to identify priorities for digitization projects and for other improved means of access to their collections. Perhaps through professional societies such as the ARLIS/NA[75] funding might be sought for cooperative ventures that would identify our unique resources, improve intellectual access to these materials, sponsor digital reformatting projects, and collocate the resulting digital surrogates in a way that facilitates access to these materials. Obvious benefits to our users will be improved access to our special collections. For our materials, the benefits should include reduced handling, and in some cases reduced need to preserve brittle copies in multiple locations. We could then concentrate our special collection management efforts and access services on our unique holdings. Without access to additional (or special project) funding, lack of appropriate staffing, time, and equipment will be major barriers to increased access and improved preservation. Technology, when affordable, should no longer be a barrier. Nevertheless, many of our special collection items are collected for their value as artifacts, and we will need to continue to preserve and service these original materials for the foreseeable future.

NOTES

1. Such collections are occasionally featured on their libraries' web sites, such as the 2,000 volume Perkins Library of rare architectural titles at the University of Pennsylvania's Fisher Fine Arts Library (http://www.library.upenn.edu/services/collections/coll-finearts.html?finearts) and the Special Collections at the University of Michigan's Media Union Library (http://www.lib.umich.edu/ummu.scdesc.html). One library even

houses a brick fragment from the destroyed Tokyo Imperial Hotel designed by Frank Lloyd Wright (See: Peggy Ann Kusnerz, ed. *The Architecture Library of the Future: Complexity and Contradiction.* Ann Arbor: The University of Michigan Press, 1989, vii.). Note: All URLs were verified in May 2002.

2. See p. 32 in: Antoinette Nelson and Polyanne Frantz, "Accessing Closed Collections: The Librarian Holds the Key," *Technical Services Quarterly*, 17, no. 1 (1999): 31-36.

3. Ann Baird Whiteside, Pamela Born, and Adeanne Alpert Bregman, comp. *Collection Development Policies for Libraries & Visual Collections in the Arts.* Occasional Paper no. 12. Laguna Beach: Art Libraries Society of North America, 2000. See p. 62 for the Boston Architectural Center Library, p. 82-83 for the Maine College of Art Library, and p. 88 for the Pratt Institute Library. The Art Libraries Society of the United Kingdom & Eire also includes archival materials and 'specialist collections' in their *Guidelines for Art and Design Libraries.* London: Art Libraries Society, 1990, 8-9, 13.

4. Jane Carlin and Adrienne Varady, "Snow Globes, Valentines, Mail Art, Oh My!: Weird and Wonderful Art Library Collections," *Art Documentation*, 18, no. 1 (Spring 1999): 46-49.

5. Ibid., 46.

6. Ibid., 49.

7. Clive Phillpot, "Flies in the Files: Ephemera in the Art Library," *Art Documentation*, 14, no. 1 (Spring 1995) 13-14.

8. Betty Jo Irvine, ed. *Facilities Standards for Art Libraries and Visual Resources Collections.* Englewood, Colorado: Libraries Unlimited, Inc., 1991.

9. College, university, research, art school, museum, public library, and visual resources collections.

10. *Facilities Standards for Art Libraries*, 118-119.

11. Ibid. See also "Appendix VI: Examples of Building Programs and Planning Documents" for examples of requirements for several branch library facilities that include rare book rooms.

12. "ACRL Guidelines for Branch Libraries in Colleges and Universities," *College & Research Libraries News*, 52, no. 3 (March 1991): 171-174. (Approved as policy by the Board of Directors of the Association of College and Research Libraries on June 26, 1990.)

13. Ibid., 172.

14. Mary Ellen Dusey, "Circulation within Special Collections and Archives," *Nebraska Library Association Quarterly*, 31, no. 3 (Spring 2000): 9-11.

15. "ACRL Guidelines for Branch Libraries," 173.

16. Susan Garretson Swartzburg, "Preservation Considerations in Developing Library Space," in *Space Planning for the Art Library.* Occasional Paper no. 9. Tucson: Art Libraries Society of North America, 1991. 17-20.

17. Carolee Parry Griffin, "A Study of Conservation/Preservation Treatment of Materials in Fine Arts Libraries," *The Georgia Librarian*, 30 (Summer 1993): 41-43.

18. Anita Vriend, "Creating Guidelines for Disaster Planning," *Art Libraries Journal*, 27, no. 1 (2002): 27-30, as well as: ARLIS/NL. *Werkgroep Calamiteitenplanning*, http://www.let.uu.nl/~okbn/activiteiten/werkgroepen/calamiteitenplanning/ (the guidelines and worksheets are in Dutch). National Library of Australia. *Disaster Planning for Libraries and Archives: Understanding the Essential Issues,* http://www.nla.gov.au/nla/staffpaper/lyall1.html.

19. Leo Shkolnik, "The Continuing Debate over Academic Branch Libraries," *College and Research Libraries*, 52, no. 4 (July 1991): 343-351.

20. Olivia M. Madison, Sally A. Frey, and David Gregory, "A Model for Reviewing Academic Branch Libraries Based on ACRL Guidelines and Standards," *College and Research Libraries*, 55, no. 4 (July 1994): 342-354.

21. Charlotte Crockett, "Reconfiguring the Branch Library for a More Virtual Future," *Library Administration & Management*, 14, no. 4 (Fall 2000): 191-196.

22. For a discussion of how artists and designers use libraries, consult: Deirdre C. Stam, "Artists and Art Libraries," *Art Libraries Journal*, 20, no. 2 (1995): 21-24, and Philip Pacey, "Demystifying Design: The Information Needs of Non-Professional Designers," *Art Libraries Journal*, 16, no. 3 (1991): 25-31.

23. *Library of Congress Prints and Photographs: An Illustrated Guide*. Washington, D.C.: Library of Congress, 1995. Also available as an online version at: http://lcweb.loc.gov/rr/print/guide.

24. For a discussion of rare book collection web sites, see: Heidi J. Dressler. *University Rare Book Collections on the Web: Analysis and Recommendations*. Thesis (MSLS) University of North Carolina at Chapel Hill, 2000.

25. For example, try searching the names 'Cret' or 'Rowe' in the Provenance (Collection) keyword field in UTNetCAT (http://utdirect.utexas.edu/lib/utnetcat/kword.html).

26. In addition to the material in our Special Collections stacks, the Architecture and Planning Library also houses a substantial collection of archival records (the Alexander Architectural Archive, currently housing approximately 70 collections that include drawings, photographic materials, files, and more). These collections are accessed by appointment through a separate public service area. More information about this material is located at http://www.lib.utexas.edu/apl/aaa/index.html.

27. This means that unlike other branches on campus, we cannot leave the library with only a single student employee in attendance. It also makes it difficult for the librarian and desk supervisors to attend the same meetings!

28. Information on user education for care and handling of special collection materials is available from: Kenneth Lavender, "Preservation Education for the Library User: The Special Collections Perspective," and Charlotte B. Brown, "Care and Handling Education for Patrons," in Jeanne M. Drewes and Julie Page, eds. *Promoting Preservation Awareness in Libraries: A Sourcebook for Academic, Public, School, and Special Collections*. Westport, CT: Greenwood Press 1997, 263-279, 285-296.

29. The books from the collection of architect Charles W. Moore are kept in their original order in his former home, on bookcases that he designed. This home is now the Charles W. Moore Center for the Study of Place (see http://www.charlesmoore.org). The library of architectural historian Colin Rowe is also one of our special collections housed in the Center. If paging of materials must be done in inclement weather (which we try to avoid), our solution has been to pack them in plastic coolers instead of boxes.

30. We have over 11,000 volumes in our Special Collections stacks plus approximately 6,000 more volumes at the Charles W. Moore Center for the Study of Place. The Special Collection materials are shelved in five different size groupings: tinies, octavos, quartos, folios, and elephant folios.

31. See http://www.lib.utexas.edu/apl/news.html.

32. Josef Albers. *Interaction of Color*. New Haven: Yale University Press, 1963. (This is the original edition with the silk-screened plates.)

33. Antoinette Nelson and Pollyanne Frantz. "Accessing Closed Collections: The Librarian Holds the Key," *Technical Services Quarterly*, 17, no. 1 (1999): 31-36.

34. Ibid., 33.

35. Daniel Starr, "Cataloging Artist Files: One Library's Approach to Providing Integrated Access to Ephemeral Material," *66th IFLA Council and General Conference, Jerusalem, Israel, 13-18 August, Conference Proceedings,* paper 068-165-E (http://www.ifla.org/IV/ifla66/papers/068-165e.htm).

36. See: *TARO: Texas Archival Resources Online* at http://www.lib.utexas.edu/taro/.

37. "ACRL Guidelines for the Preparation of Policies on Library Access: A Draft," Prepared by the ACRL Access Policy Guidelines Task Force, *College & Research Libraries News,* 53, no. 11 (December 1992): 709-718.

38. Megan Mulder, "Just Say No?: Special Collections and Interlibrary Loan," *North Carolina Libraries,* 53 (Fall 1995): 113-115.

39. See: http://etext.lib.virginia.edu/.

40. Mulder, "Just Say No?": 114.

41. Ibid., 113-115, and "Draft Guidelines for the Loan of Rare and Unique Materials," *College & Research Libraries News,* 54 (May 1993): 5, 267-269. One non-circulating collection reports that the advantage of not participating in interlibrary loan arrangements is that all of its materials are available to researchers at the institution.

42. Gallagher, Connell B. "Resources Sharing Among Archival Institutions and Special Collections: Focus on the User While Protecting the Collection," *Mississippi Libraries,* 58, no. 4 (Winter 1994): 93-95.

43. See: http://lcweb.loc.gov/rr/loan/illscanhome.html.

44. For their digital scanning policy, see: http://www.lsu.edu/special/frames/services.html.

45. David Cobb, "Limits to Access–You can Look But Don't Touch." *67th IFLA Council and General Conference, August 16-25, 2001,* paper 174-166-E (http://www.ifla.org/IV/ifla67/papers/174-166e.pdf).

46. Ibid.

47. Leslie A. Morris, "Beyond the Books: Programs for Exhibitions," *Rare Books and Manuscripts Librarianship,* 6, no. 2 (1999): 89-99.

48. See: http://www.tulane.edu/~lmiller/SEAAAHome.html.

49. Alison Minns, "Never Judge a Book by Its Cover," *Library Association Record,* 98 (Sept. 1996): 474-476.

50. Additional public relations activities are outlined in the "Public Relations" chapter in: A. M. Scham. *Managing Special Collections.* New York: Neal-Schuman Publishers, 1987: 78-87. Scham believes that "it is the task of curators of special collections to make known their holdings and to attract scholars and students."

51. National Information Standards Organization (U.S.). *Environmental Conditions for Exhibiting Library and Archival Materials.* "ANSI/NISO Z39.79-2001" Bethesda, MD: NISO Press, 2001. (Also available through http://www.niso.org.) In addition, Colorado College staff prepared a useful list of conservation techniques to keep in mind while mounting special collection exhibits and Pamela Barrios published instructions for easy to make book supports (as well as handy tips for photography from books). See: Christine Erdmann. *Special Collections in College Libraries.* CLIP Notes no. 6. Chicago: American Library Association, 1986: 84-85, and Pamela Barrios, "Simplifying the Problems of Conservation in Exhibitions," *Rare Books and Manuscripts Librarianship,* 12, no. 2 (1998): 78-85.

52. "Guidelines for Borrowing Special Collections Materials for Exhibitions," *College & Research Libraries News,* 5 (May 1990): 430-434. These guidelines recom-

mend a minimum of six months lead-time for loan requests (more if conservation work is required).

53. For examples of this, see *Blake's Choice* at the University of Texas at Austin (http://www.lib.utexas.edu/apl/blakeschoice/index.html) and the University of Delaware's *Personal Visions: Artists' Books at the Millennium* (http://www.lib.udel.edu/ud/spec/exhibits/artistsbook/index.html).

54. See p. 236 in: Peter A. Graham, "New Roles for Special Collections on the Network," *College and Research Libraries*, 59, no. 3 (May 1998): 232-239.

55. For a study of the motivations behind this phenomenon, see: Nancy J. Kaiser. *Diffusion of Innovations in Special Collections Libraries: The Motivations Behind Adoption of Digitization.* Thesis (MSLS) University of North Carolina at Chapel Hill, 2000. That special collections librarians are interested in taking on these challenges is evidenced by their attendance at workshops and special training sessions such as the one reported on in "Yesterdays and Tomorrow: The Digitization of Library Special Collections," *Multimedia Information and Technology*, 25, no. 3 (August 1999): 254-255.

56. Peter B. Hirtle, "The Impact of Digitization on Special Collections in Libraries," *Libraries and Culture*, 37, no. 1 (Winter 2002): 42-52.

57. Ibid., 47.

58. Ibid., 49.

59. Ibid., 50.

60. See for instance: Robert James Coote, *The Eclectic Odyssey of Atlee B. Ayres, Architect.* College Station: Texas A&M University Press, 2001. Professor Coote made heavy use of archival and special collection materials housed in the Architecture and Planning Library at the University of Texas at Austin. These archival records include information about the date of purchase of many books in the Ayres library and the books themselves show much evidence of their use.

61. Graham, "New Roles," 233.

62. Josef Albers. *Interaction of Color.* Interactive CD-ROM ed. New Haven: Yale University Press, 1994.

63. Graham, "New Roles," 234.

64. See: http://www.rlg.org/longterm/repositories.pdf.

65. See: http://www.chartingthenation.lib.ed.ac.uk.

66. See: http://www.columbia.edu/cu/libraries/inside/projects/greene_and_greene/.

67. See p. 25 of: Jennifer Durran, "Art History, Scholarship and Image Libraries: Realising the Potential of the Digital Age," *LASIE*, 28 (June 1997): 14-27.

68. See: http://decorativearts.library.wisc.edu. Among the electronic facsimiles available from the Wisconsin site are several builder's guides and painting treatises.

69. See: http://dl.tamu.edu/aggiana/collections/texshare/home.html and Beth M. Russell, "From the Ground Up: Lessons Learned from a Librarian's Experience with Digitizing Special Collections," *College & Research Libraries News*, 62, no. 6 (June 2001): 603-606.

70. See: Robert S. Martin and Faye Phillips, "Scanning Historical Documents: The Electronic Imaging Laboratory at Louisiana State University," *Journal of Education for Library and Information Science*, 34 (Fall 1993): 298-301. Faye Philips and Richard Condrey, "Louisiana State University Libraries' Electronic Imaging Laboratory," *Microform Review*, 23 (Winter 1994): 26-28. Richard Condrey and Faye Phillips, "Preservation Through Reformatting: An Update on the LSU Libraries Electronic Imaging Laboratory," *LLA Bulletin*, 55 (Spring 1993): 235-237. Richard Condrey,

Faye Phillips, and Tony Presti, "Historical Ecology: LSU's Electronic Imaging Laboratory," *College & Research Libraries News*, 54, no. 8 (Sept. 1993): 438, 441, 448.

71. For instance, *Trade Catalogues from the Avery Library, Columbia University*. Frederick, MD: UPA Academic Editions, 1989 (3,477 microfiche) and *The Museum of Modern Art Artists Files*. Alexandria, VA: Chadwyck-Healy, 1986 (5,699 microfiche).

72. See: http://gerritsen.chadwyck.com/.

73. Simon Ford, "The Disorder of Things: The Postmodern Art Library," *Art Libraries Journal*, 18, no. 3 (1993): 10-23.

74. Graham, "New Roles," 235.

75. See: http://www.arlisna.org/.

THE BIG PICTURE:
COMPARING PRACTICES
IN ART LIBRARIES

Patrons, Processes, and the Profession: Comparing the Academic Art Library and the Art Museum Library

Kim Collins

SUMMARY. Much has been written about the difference between academic art historians and art museum scholars, but what about the libraries that support these patrons? College and university libraries hold a special position at the heart of their institutions; art museum libraries struggle to stay relevant in more peripheral roles. On the other hand, aca-

Kim Collins is Art History Librarian, Emory University in Atlanta, GA. She also worked for several years as the head librarian at the High Museum of Art Library, Atlanta, GA, and has served as an adjunct faculty member at Clark Atlanta University's School of Library Science, teaching a class on art librarianship.

[Haworth co-indexing entry note]: "Patrons, Processes, and the Profession: Comparing the Academic Art Library and the Art Museum Library." Collins, Kim. Co-published simultaneously in *Journal of Library Administration* (The Haworth Information Press, an imprint of The Haworth Press, Inc.) Vol. 39, No. 1, 2003, pp. 77-89; and: *The Twenty-First Century Art Librarian* (ed: Terrie L. Wilson) The Haworth Information Press, an imprint of The Haworth Press, Inc., 2003, pp. 77-89. Single or multiple copies of this article are available for a fee from The Haworth Document Delivery Service [1-800-HAWORTH, 9:00 a.m. - 5:00 p.m. (EST). E-mail address: docdelivery@haworth press.com].

http://www.haworthpress.com/store/product.asp?sku=J111
10.1300/J111v39n01_05

demic art librarians, whether working in an art library branch or within the main library, must compete with other research disciplines in a manner unfamiliar to art museum librarians. This article attempts to compare the two types of libraries, focusing on issues of patrons, funding priorities, material budgets, library marketing, technical infrastructure, and professional development. *[Article copies available for a fee from The Haworth Document Delivery Service: 1-800-HAWORTH. E-mail address: <docdelivery@haworth press.com> Website: <http://www.HaworthPress.com> © 2003 by The Haworth Press, Inc. All rights reserved.]*

KEYWORDS. Art librarianship, art library, art libraries, art historians, art history, art museum curators, academic art libraries, museum libraries, research methods, budgeting, collection development, marketing, patrons, professional development

DEFINING THE ART HISTORIAN AND OTHER ART LIBRARY PATRONS

Art libraries have a myriad of patrons, but their most targeted users are art historians. On the surface, art historians who teach at universities and those who work as museum curators seem very similar. Both have upper level degrees (usually PhDs) in their field and have demonstrated considerable expertise on researching and writing about art. However, in the past decade, much has been written about the contrasting roles of academic art historians and art museum curators. Exploring these differences helps define the research needs of these art historians and illuminates the possible divergent focus of the academic and museum art libraries.

Richard Brillant argued in 1992 that while both parties begin with the art object their interests diverge with the presentation of information.[1] The academic tends to produce scholarly monographs and the curator exhibition-cum-catalogue.[2] According to Brillant, the curator must act as a "collector, guarantor of authenticity, conservator, inventory manager, recorder, journalist, exhibitor, and asset protector and enhancer."[3] How then can curators find time to produce scholarly-critical writing that includes a historical perspective on an artwork? This is especially difficult when they must also strive to educate a public with a very varied knowledge base and facilitate a direct experience with the art for the museum visitor.

Ivan Gaskell writes that academic art historians (mostly teachers in tertiary education) are the critical essayists and theorists, while art museum scholars are practical critics that put their judgement into predominantly physical, rather than written, form.[4] He equates this comparison to one between a university medical professor and a physician or surgeon. For the museum curator, the research and documentation of visual material (i.e., writing about art) is secondary to presenting the visual.

Museums, often portrayed as money-grubbing and quick to compromise, get criticized for producing crowd-pleasing, blockbuster exhibitions. Yet, these shows do bring people through the doors and further the institution's educational mission. Of course, this teaching role can also be (and often is) taken to the extreme. While educating the public seems like a very noble cause, James Cuno contends that the image of the 'museum as social institution' challenges its scholarly mission even more than the perception that museums are too market driven.[5] Not only are museums mandated to educate the public to appreciate the visual arts, they are encouraged to "help nurture a humane citizenry equipped to make informed choices in a democracy and to address challenges and opportunities in an increasingly global society."[6] Such a broad focus can only dilute scholarship.

'New' art history is interdisciplinary and revisionist, drawing on methods from many fields and questioning the formal canons of the past. While the academic curriculum embraces this more theoretical approach, museums seem to be dragging their feet, perhaps with good reason. The Smithsonian Institution's 1992 revisionist exhibit, *The West as America: Reinterpreting Images of the Frontier, 1820-1920*, raised eyebrows and incited passions. The curator of the controversial exhibition challenged a mainly non-academic audience to reexamine beloved pictures of the American West, asking them to take into account the negative aspects of western expansion and to question the underlying ideology of the images. While these ideas hardly seem revolutionary in an academic setting, the museum public found them very jarring. *The West as America* was a perfect example of 'new' art history applied to the museum arena; it utilized physical art objects, paintings, to address complex issues. The most telling fallout is that the exhibition catalogue, primarily about physical art works and produced by an art museum, was originally catalogued by the Library of Congress under the F class (US geography) rather than the ND class (painting).

James Cuno concludes that money must be allocated for museums to produce and distribute scholarship: "Spending today's money for tomorrow's benefit."[7] Indeed, over the past decade, the general public does seem to have become more accepting of this type of critical approach to producing exhibits. The recent exhibition proposal, *The Spirit of America,* was lambasted for being too commemorative and not critical enough. Museum art librarians need to promote the connection that a well-maintained museum library will enable curators to conduct in-depth research that will lead to more provocative, scholarly exhibitions. Of course, museums want to fight the stereotype of being elitist and "academic," but why can't entertainment be scholarly and the scholarly entertaining?[8]

We can define the two types of art historians, but how does this process help differentiate the academic art library from its museum counterpart? In the mid-eighties, art librarian Deirdre Stam conducted a groundbreaking empirical study of both academic and museum art historians with hopes to improve library services for these patrons.[9] In the simplest terms, both types of scholars interpret an art object in light of existing information and original observation. They make frequent use of libraries (although not necessarily librarians) and often travel for research purposes. Their search for bibliographic material, including accidental discovery associated with the search process, is crucial to their final product. Stam's study seems to indicate that the two types of patrons are really more similar than dissimilar. At least they are more closely related to each other, than say a typical patron of an art and design school library.[10] More recently, Ronald de Leeuw has promoted the mutual dependence of academics and curators.[11] The museum benefits from trying to interpret art historical theory and the university art historian profits from an increased interest in contextuality. In any event, both academic art libraries and art museum libraries must provide extensive collections for a very library-savvy audience.

As mentioned above, while art historians are important users of art libraries, they are far from the only patrons. An academic art library caters to students. Of course, the primary student user group is composed of art history undergraduates, graduates, and studio art majors. However, it should not be forgotten that art books and resources are very popular with students from other disciplines and the public at large.

The museum library must also support staff from museum departments other than curatorial, such as education, public relations, development, and administration. To support the museum's education department, art librarians need ready-reference for training docents, as well as age-specific material for teachers of all grade levels. Development requires resources on foundations, grants, and donors. Administration needs comparative data published on other museums and publications from various museum and art associations. Also, like the academic art library, the art museum library often serves the general public. Of course, few art museum libraries circulate their material to individuals outside of immediate museum staff members.

COLLECTION DEVELOPMENT

While scholarly monographs, important exhibition catalogues, and art journals make up the majority of the collection for both university and museum art libraries, each has some unique material worth mentioning, especially since its inclusion or exclusion in a collection reflects a library's budget priorities. For example, art museum libraries are much more likely than academic art libraries to collect full-runs of auction catalogues. These lavishly illustrated sale catalogues are viewed by curators (in their role as 'collector') before the auctions and then kept by the library for patrons to use while researching provenance, conducting appraisals, or simply locating color images of artists' works. Academic art historians sometimes need this type of "image-centric" information too but often must travel to the museum library to retrieve it.[12] Many museum art libraries keep vertical artist files. The material found in artist files, such as artist pamphlets and exhibition brochures, is inexpensive (usually sent for free or as part of an exchange program), but the labor cost of maintaining such a resource is very high. Academic art libraries have a harder time getting this type of ephemeral material and do not seem to have the inclination to devote the staff time needed to create and maintain such files. Museum art libraries also collect educational material produced by the museum staff and other resources for the public, such as art books geared for children, which would be inappropriate for an academic art library.

Both libraries purchase the twenty to thirty core art journals, including *Art Bulletin, Art Journal, Art in America, Art Forum, ArtNews,* etc. Yet, generally, university art libraries subscribe to more journals, covering broader subject areas. Their journal lists include titles on popular culture and scholarly writings. Museum libraries tend to focus on pockets of specialized journals mirroring their collection of artwork. Both must also purchase catalogue raisonnés, despite the expense.

Because many museums participate in exchange programs, the art museum library has more exhibition catalogues in their collection than the academic art library. In fact, museum libraries often have very obscure material from around the world that has never been made available for sale.

The academic art library is more likely to collect extensive special collections and expensive microform products. Also, the academic institution usually has more funds than a museum library to purchase electronic art resources, including indexing databases, full-text e-resources, and e-journals. Indeed, most museum libraries are considerably behind their university counterpoints when it comes to technology and subscriptions to electronically available information. In the past, researchers relied heavily on finding material through the bibliographies of their colleagues' published writings. Today, however, many patrons, especially art history curators recently graduated from academic universities, are demanding that priority be given to purchasing electronic databases. Partnerships and consortiums are usually the only hope for art museum libraries to gain access to these electronic resources.

Will technology change the character of either type of library? Investing in technology does reduce the funds available to purchase print resources, but, so far, it has failed to quench patrons' desire or need for the art book. If vendors can solve the cost, copyright, quality, and disk-space problems associated with presenting images in their electronic databases, technology might play a greater role in future art history research. Likewise, the emerging cataloging standards for visual images will greatly increase access to digitized artwork and might have an impact on scholarship in the field. Perhaps it is still too early to tell. Of course, technology has already increased the speed of research and made some new comparisons more possible. Paul Greenhalgh cautions in his article, "The Art Library–A Moving Target" (1995), that technology cannot deliver "historical truth or philosophical soundness"; it can just speed up the research process. Now, scholars can produce rubbish at five times the speed.[13] Another consequence is that technology reduces the number of patrons who actually walk through the door of art libraries. Statistically this might appear worrisome, but a satisfied patron is a satisfied patron. In fact, patrons who are able to find answers from their own desktop or from simply e-mailing a librarian almost always remain loyal supporters of the library.

BUDGET PRIORITIES AND FUNDING STRATEGIES

As mentioned above, the academic library usually has a more central, established position within the parent organization than the museum library. However, now more than ever, both types of art libraries must build a case for continued growth. It seems universal that librarians dislike the term, "marketing"–and art librarians are no exception. However, Marylaine Block makes a good case for it in her article, "The Secret of Library Marketing: Make Yourself Indispensable."[14] She writes that librarians must convince the local power structure that they are the "go-to" people for information, ferreting out their patrons' information needs before they even vocalize them. Librarians should not settle for being good at what they do but must strive to be *known* to be good at what they do. How does this relate to budgets? Well, the budget process also involves strategic planning (i.e., understanding priorities, values, and commitments). William David Penniman writes that the first step in the budget process is to ask whether issues important to the library are also important to the funding body.[15] The museum art librarian must continually justify budget requests and explain funding priorities to an administration that probably does not understand how libraries are run. An academic art librarian is usually proposing budgets to a library administrator. (Of course, the library director must in turn convince the university dean, who may or may not have any in-depth knowledge of library administration.) Suffice to say that the academic art librarian usually has a more educated funding body, although not necessarily a more sympathetic one. As Murray Martin summarizes, "the primary need for a budget is to persuade those responsible for receiving the request that the facts presented are correct, that the conclusions drawn are reasonable, and the goals underlying the budget are acceptable."[16] This advice works for both types of art libraries. However, while it is always wise to avoid library jargon when presenting a budget to a funding body, the art museum librarian will probably have to spend more time defining basic library concepts than the academic art librarian does.

Another key to a successful budget presentation is demonstrating a proven track record. This is especially true for the museum library administrator who must constantly justify expenses. Indeed, the notion of accountability probably comes up more in the museum environment than the academic library. That being said, universities are now also beginning to view their libraries with a more business-like orientation. While in theory the academic art library has a more secure position in the university than the art library has within the museum, the current economic downturn makes the budget process challenging for all types of libraries. And, simply relying on what worked in the past can be treacherous. Douglas Birdsall writes, "any posturing about the library's special place on campus or its inherent value will not serve the [academic library] director well in today's economic environment."[17] Instead, the director should make the budget case on programmatic links to the university's mission and goals. Likewise, the museum librarian must convince the director that the curatorial, education, development, public relations, and publication departments of the museum will fail to accomplish their mission without the library's resources and services.

How then can art librarians effect change when it comes to the budget process? Sheila D. Creth does a wonderful job of outlining several assumptions influencing funding allocations that librarians should question and perhaps even challenge.[18] The first is the validity, even sanctity, of statistics and formulas. Academic librarians are much more likely to fall into this trap than museum librarians, partially because of institutional culture and partially because short-staffed museum librarians often don't have the time, money, or skill to create such complex analyses. Creth warns that statistics can lead to the "bigger is better" syndrome and/or a "protect & defend" mentality. Neither is very helpful in the long-run. Instead, the budget allocations should reflect that the library is "not only being efficient (i.e., costs are contained or reduced as feasible) but that [the library is] also being effective (i.e., that we are doing the right things)."[19] Likewise, both museum and academic libraries should address the access-versus-ownership question. In the past, budget limitations forced many art museum libraries to partner with other institutions to achieve such basic goals as library automation. Now, both types of libraries are reexamining the "just in case" principle and opting for more collaborative and consortial arrangements. Art historians tend to be heavy inter-library loan users anyway and are accustomed to the patience required to utilize this service. However, because many art museum libraries are non-circulating, they have to establish relationships with other institutions or consortiums in order to take advantage of the inter-library loan option for their patrons. This type of arrangement usually does carry some budget repercussions.

To summarize, the academic art library must continually link its material budget to university programs and priorities, while maintaining a general fund for broad coverage and special purchasing opportunities. Electronic resources, especially in fields other than art, continue to consume larger and larger portions of the academic library's budget. The art museum library will continue to rely on the exchange program to supplement their acquisitions budgets, although art librarians are becoming increasingly frustrated with the additional staff time it takes to maintain these programs. Museum libraries that are non-circulating can have a more focused collecting policy, but rarely does this relieve any budget constraints. Their main priorities must be to collect actively in fields tied to their permanent collection and to collect very wisely on subjects related to traveling exhibitions. The latter requires great diplomacy as the museum curator and educator might not be sympathetic, or even aware, of the library's big budget picture.

ENVIRONMENT AND INSTITUTIONAL CULTURE

Museum art libraries usually operate with less manpower and lag behind on technical innovations. The golden lining is that their smaller size gives the library more flexibility. Also, this lag allows them to bypass some technical hurdles, waiting for larger academic libraries to work out all the kinks in new software and other technical products. Of course, while a university can be large and cumbersome, it usually has the funding and adequate technical support to be on the cutting edge.

These two types of libraries also have different work cycles. The academic art library is busiest during the school year. The beginning and end of semesters (or quarters) are always stressful. Also, academic librarians can usually recruit student help during these months and major projects do get accomplished. The art museum librarian has a more even-keel year, often experiencing a spike in activity during the summer months. This is the time when curators can devote more time to their scholarly research. Likewise, the art museum library often gets additional volunteer help from summer interns and docents (who experience a lull in tour activity during the times that the schools are out of session).

While academic librarians prefer to compare their salaries, benefits, and university standing with faculty, the art museum librarian struggles to maintain equity with the museum curator. Both kinds of librarians face frustration and must constantly "market" the professional comparison. Many academic art librarians even go through the tenure process. Museums usually do not have such a formal structure, but it is still very important that the librarian get involved with the issues of the institution as a whole. The art library, whether in a museum or an academic environment, might be an oasis but it cannot remain an island. Both types of art librarians must interact frequently and effectively with their parent organization in order to maintain influence and justify their positions. This could mean attending meetings, publishing highlights of new library material, or even providing proactive reference services or acquisitions.

PROFESSIONAL DEVELOPMENT

In any field, professional excellence is linked to continued learning. This is especially true for the information specialist. Professional development can entail reading current professional literature, attending conferences, and networking with colleagues. Art librarians in the United States (and the United Kingdom) have their own professional organization, the Art Libraries Society (of North America or United Kingdom, respectively).[20] Many North American art librarians also participate in the American Libraries Association and the Special Libraries Association. For the academic art librarian, the professional organization provides an opportunity to build a resume, publish, demonstrate teamwork, and develop leadership skills. The art museum librarian also benefits from the list above but seems most interested in learning about what other colleagues are doing. To this end, the conference is paramount. Yet, before extolling the many virtues of the professional conference, it seems worth mentioning some of the limitations. Phyllis DiBianco in her article, "The Changing Face of Professional Development," argues that librarians need to rely more heavily on the Internet to improve their professional practice. The Internet (including listservs, etc.) offers an increasing amount of information for the professional who actively seeks learning experiences, without the frustrations of the conference experience. DiBianco reminisces:

> We would check the calendars of our regional, state, and national associations, identify conferences and workshops we want to attend, submit approval forms, hold our breaths while conference budgets were checked–and then off we would go. We would return dazed and exhausted, carrying a new logo'd bag laden with brochures, catalogs, our copious notes, and high expectations of doing things differently. In thinking back, we realize that after using those notes to write required conference reports, our high expectations for change and improvement faded over time. Such was the staff development cycle. What was wrong with this picture? Plenty!: For one thing, our collection of conference bags grew at an exponential rate while our learning curve did not.[21]

Most professional librarians can identify with the frustrations of "company" travel and the information-overload syndrome described above. In response, many art librarians have become very active on list-serves, such as ARLIS-L,[22] and have chosen to forgo the annual conference experience. That being said, nothing can serve as a substitute for attending programs and workshops, visiting the exhibit hall to talk with vendors, and chatting with colleagues face-to-face. For the solo museum librarian, a conference or chapter meeting might be the only opportunity to interact with other professionals. (Solo academic art librarians can usually walk across campus to contact other librarians, even if they work with other disciplines.) Something must also be said for the jolt a conference can bring to one's day-to-day operations. Being inundated with new ideas can be stressful but also exhilarating. No one can retain all the information they receive at a conference, but being exposed to ideas and networking with colleagues should allow one to retrieve the information again when it is needed back at the home institution. Being inspired by a challenge, even an unobtainable one, can spark positive change. When art librarians work on committees or serve as leaders within a professional organization, they are building management skills. The Association of College and Research Libraries (ACRL) states that "academic and research librarians have a responsibility to share what they have learned through writing, speaking, mentoring, and modeling, in order to facilitate the learning of their colleagues and the advancement of the profession."[23] Art librarians, both those from academic institutions and from museums, are very fortunate to have vibrant organizations, such as ARLIS/NA and ARLIS/UK, which can help accomplish this goal.

Funding for professional development varies widely from institution to institution. Academic librarians should have access to more money for travel; however, this is not always the case. Universities must draft reimbursement policies that apply to all professional employees, often limiting amounts to unrealistic caps that force art librarians to contribute personal funds to attend conferences. Smaller museums can be more flexible with funding for travel and continuing education. Of course, having the desire to support the museum's professional staff does not always translate to having the money available for professional development. If the museum administration is repeatedly convinced of the value of having their librarian(s) attend a professional conference, they can budget for it. Often museums compromise by sending only one representative and relying on that individual to share information with the rest of the library staff. Universities could also adopt this policy in regards to conferences. With other professional development such as classes and workshops, academic librarians seem to get more support than art museum librarians. Because of the culture of their institution, they probably have an easier time justifying money spent on continuing education, such as on-line courses, distance learning opportunities, and local seminars.

CONCLUSION

The patrons of academic art libraries and art museum libraries might have different needs and "products," but they both rely on research conducted in the library. The emphasis of the collections might be different, but the services and technical infrastructure needed to maintain the two libraries are very similar. They differ slightly in their relation to the parent organization. Universities' central mission of research places the academic library in good standing. Art museums also strive to educate and enlighten, but scholarly research has been relegated to a more auxiliary position. The art museum librarian must constantly convince their administration that access to scholarly research is a "must-have" not just a nice benefit. Luckily, most art historians are also strong library advocates. Both types of art librarians are charged with the goal of lifetime learning. Museums and universities need to recognize their role in the continued professional development of their librarians. Lastly, art librarians need to constantly champion the library to patrons and administrators. The profession depends on committed members who can influence funding allocations, create library users and resource needs, and mentor a new generation of art librarians to work in our universities and art museums.

NOTES AND REFERENCES

1. Richard Brillant, "Out of Site, Out of Mind," *Art Bulletin* 74: 4 (December 1992) p. 551.

2. Over the past decade since Brillant's controversial editorial, exhibition catalogues have continued to evolve into ambitious, weighty tomes, sometimes packed with scholarly research, other times just slick and expensive. Ronald de Leeuw points out in his article, "The History of art between the 20th and 21st century," *Diogenes* 47:1 (1999), that because of high print runs, popular focus, and deadline pressures, the museum exhibition catalogue is very useful and inexpensive tool for art historians (both academic and museum scholars) to publish their ideas quickly.

3. Brillant, p. 551.

4. Ivan Gaskell, "Writing (and) Art History: Against Writing," *Art Bulletin* 78:3 (September 96) p. 403.

5. James Cuno, "Whose Money? Whose Power?, Whose Art History?" *Art Bulletin* 79:1 (March 1997).

6. *Excellence and Equity: Education and the Public Dimension of Museums, a Report from the American Association of Museums*, Washington D.C., 1992, p. 6.

7. Ibid.

8. The museum scholar will need to promote this type of critical writing to the public and to other museum professionals. We all know 'sleeper' exhibitions that

failed to excite the museum's PR department or to secure funds for a flashy catalogue, yet with worthy art and solid curatorial research, won the hearts of the museum-going audience.

9. See Deirdre Stam, "How Art Historians Look for Information," *Art Documentation,* 3 (Winter 1984) p. 117-119 and Deirdre Stam, "Tracking Art Historians: On Information Needs and Information-seeking Behavior," *Art Libraries Journal* 14:3 (1989), p. 13-16.

10. Philip Pacey provides an accurate and entertaining look at the library needs of the art and design school student in his classic article, "How art students use libraries–if they do" *Art Libraries Journal* 7(Spring 1982) p. 33-38.

11. de Leeuw, p. 78-82.

12. Many academic art libraries only collect a few auction catalogues which they often treat like monographs. Perhaps electronic database projects will eventually make this information more readily available to the academic art historian but digitizing so many color images is costly (and technologically difficult). Likewise, academic libraries are currently unwilling to allocate much money for this type of reference tool.

13. Paul Greenhalgh, "The Art Library–A Moving Target," *Art Libraries Journal* 20/2 (1995) p. 17.

14. Marylaine Block, "The Secret of Library Marketing: Make Yourself Indispensable," *American Libraries* 32 (September 2001) p. 48-50.

15. W. David Penniman (William David), "Funding Priorities and Funding Strategies (of the Council on Library Resources)" *Applying Research to Practice: How to Use Data Collection and Research to Improve Library Management Decision Making.* Allerton Park Institute (33rd: 1991: Monticello, Ill.) p. 158-166.

16. Martin S. Murray, *Academic Library Budgets* (Greenwich, CT: JAI Press, 1993) p. 118.

17. Douglas G. Birdsall, "The Micropolitics of Budgeting in Universities: Lessons for Library Administrators," *Journal of Academic Librarianship* 21 (November 1995) p. 432.

18. Sheila D. Creth, "An Academic Librarian's Response," *Library Administration and Management* 6 (Summer 1992) p. 133-140.

19. Ibid., p. 135.

20. Wolfgang Freitag gives a detailed and entertaining recount of how ARLIS/NA was founded in the article, "ARLIS/NA at Twenty-five: A Reminiscence," *Art Documentation* 16/2 (1997) p. 15-19.

21. Phyllis DiBanco, "The Changing Face of Professional Development," *Information Searcher: A Newsletter for Teaching Online Searching* 12:3 (2000) p. 12.

22. *ARLIS-L is an electronic forum for the dissemination of information and the discussion of issues of interest to art information professionals. Postings routinely include job vacancy announcements; conference, workshop, and meeting information; announcements of awards, honors, and prizes; news items from groups and individuals in the Society; new publications and web sites; copyright and information policy issues; and more . . . Anyone may subscribe by sending an e-mail message to listserv@lsv.uky.edu with the subject line blank. In the body of your message, type ONLY the following (no signature): SUBSCRIBE ARLIS-L YOUR NAME (substituting your own name).

23. "ACRL Statement on Professional Development: Approved by the ACRL Board of Directors on July 8, 2000" *C&RL News* 61 (November 2000) p. 934.

Survey of Current Practices
in Art and Architecture Libraries

Susan Craig

SUMMARY. This article will report on the responses to a survey of current practices from more than 163 art and architecture libraries in the U.S. and Canada. The October 2001 survey asked about facilities, services, equipment, acquisitions practices, collections, and library instructional activities. The surveys were sent to 195 libraries in colleges and universities, art schools, and large art museums. With an 84% response rate, this survey is one of the most comprehensive assessments of art and architecture libraries ever done. It not only provides documentation as to the state of the profession at the beginning of the twenty-first century but also will serve as a measure for art and architecture librarians to use in reviewing their own libraries. *[Article copies available for a fee from The Haworth Document Delivery Service: 1-800-HAWORTH. E-mail address: <docdelivery@haworthpress.com> Website: <http://www.HaworthPress.com> © 2003 by The Haworth Press, Inc. All rights reserved.]*

KEYWORDS. Art libraries, surveys, museum libraries, library instruction, digital image collections, library facilities

Susan Craig is Head of the Murphy Art & Architecture Library, University of Kansas, 1425 Jayhawk Boulevard, Lawrence, KS 66045.

Research support for this project was supplied by the University of Kansas Libraries Research Fund.

[Haworth co-indexing entry note]: "Survey of Current Practices in Art and Architecture Libraries." Craig, Susan. Co-published simultaneously in *Journal of Library Administration* (The Haworth Information Press, an imprint of The Haworth Press, Inc.) Vol. 39, No. 1, 2003, pp. 91-107; and: *The Twenty-First Century Art Librarian* (ed: Terrie L. Wilson) The Haworth Information Press, an imprint of The Haworth Press, Inc., 2003, pp. 91-107. Single or multiple copies of this article are available for a fee from The Haworth Document Delivery Service [1-800-HAWORTH, 9:00 a.m. - 5:00 p.m. (EST). E-mail address: docdelivery@haworthpress.com].

INTRODUCTION

Art and architecture libraries are special places. They provide the link between art objects, buildings, descriptions, criticism, reproductions, and history. These libraries are filled with documentation on art and architecture in the form of books, journals, videos, CD-ROMs, microforms, and Internet workstations. They offer premier examples of diversity as they promote the study of art, crafts, design, and architecture produced by people of every ethnicity and every age.

One of the unique aspects of art, architecture, and design collections is that textual information and visual information are equally critical. Researchers need to find a wide variety of illustrations to document, compare, and inspire. Another characteristic is that older publications remain valuable even as new resources are available. Not only is some information timeless in its significance, it may also be essential for a student to understand contemporary reaction to a building from 1880, an artist working in 1950, or a design that inspired an art movement. Sources written decades or centuries after the piece is created will reflect attitudes and artistic judgments that have changed since the origin of the object. What was controversial and challenging may have evolved into the norm and the impact of the work will best be understood by reading original sources. It is also important to remember that art, architecture, and design areas are subject to international research so sources may be in a multiplicity of languages. Scholars do not limit themselves only to studying and writing about art from their own countries or their own time but are free to examine crafts, buildings, sculpture, or painting from any region and any era.

In the 2001-02 academic year, I was granted a 5-month sabbatical leave from the University of Kansas Libraries to study the "current, best practices" in art and architecture libraries. Although I have remained professionally active throughout my 30-year career as an art librarian by attending conferences, reading appropriate publications, and networking with colleagues, I knew that some of my practices and policies for running a branch art and architecture library have been shaped by instinct and available resources rather than by research. I knew that by taking a break from my usual responsibilities and focusing on learning from colleagues in art and architecture libraries across the U.S. and Canada, I would learn new approaches to common problems.

I used two approaches to assess "current, best practices." The first was to prepare a survey instrument that would focus on four areas: library instructional programs; library space; incorporation of digital image projects into collections; and changes to collection development and acquisitions due to the Internet. For each of the four areas, I prepared several questions that I thought reflected current practice on the topic and under each question tried to include the appropriate options. It was important to me that the questions were relevant to most if not all the libraries included in the survey, transcending any limitations of collection size, location, or institutional affiliation. I tried not to repeat the same question under different areas of the instrument since I personally find that survey practice particularly annoying. I also wanted to make the questions easy to answer with a predominance of yes/no or multiple choice options. I did not want to ask colleagues to find specific budget or collection facts or to prepare lengthy written responses since I knew these options would lower the return rate. Having wide participation in the survey was an important goal. My next step was to prepare a mailing list derived from the ARLIS/NA membership, the ARL membership, and the library consortium membership for my institution, the Greater Western Library Alliance (formerly the Big 12 Plus Libraries Consortium). I made the decision that the majority of the libraries I queried would be academic libraries, especially those similar to my own institution, but I would also include large art museum libraries and art and design school libraries. I did not include public libraries or firm libraries, and I chose to only send one survey to each institution even when the institution might have had multiple units providing art and architecture collections. After finalizing the survey questions and the mailing list, I produced the survey using different colored paper for each type-of-library. By using the colored paper I could easily tally each question by type-of-library as well as by total responses. Finally I included self-addressed and stamped envelopes (even acquiring Canadian postage stamps for my northern colleagues) as a further incentive to return the survey. I also discretely numbered each survey so I could track who had responded. I included in my budget and schedule a second mailing to the non-respondents. The preparation and follow-up resulted in a high rate of return with 163 surveys returned out of 195 mailed for an 84% response.

My second research strategy was to conduct site visits to a number of art and architecture libraries in order to visit with the librarians and to see the space. In two major trips I visited art and architecture libraries at 12 universities and 7 art museums and talked personally to more than 50 librarians about their collections, policies, and practices. Although this article is not focused on these visits, I know that those discussions and observations have shaped my interpretation of the survey results.

The charts that follow reflect the survey results for each question. In most cases there are four columns indicating the three different types-of-libraries as well as the total response. I have included tallies for "No Answer" for each question since that sometimes was an important factor in understanding the counts. When respondents provided their own wording or marked multiple options when only one was requested, I have included those answers in the chart. When the question required an essay response, I have presented the replies by type-of-library but I have not indicated all the times when multiple institutions offered the same reply. As with many surveys, the free text responses are among the most interesting. For the final question I organized the answers by type-of-library and then subdivided by broad subject categories.

CONCLUSIONS

The survey provides an abundance of information about multiple aspects of art and architecture libraries. From it, we learn that our libraries share similar concerns in these early years of the 21st century:

- Lack of space to house our collections is alarming. Frequently the space solution is to store large portions of the collections off-site or in compact shelving making browsing the physical piece in order to locate the exact image or detail difficult or even impossible.
- Our libraries are offering a variety of services and equipment including reference through various delivery options, instruction, workstations, and reproduction equipment.
- Approval plans as well as individual firm orders are used extensively to acquire new mainstream publications as well as exhibition catalogs.
- Electronic books are not yet a major format for art and architecture topics although many academic institutions offer a netLibrary package.
- Although use of the Internet to find out-of-print materials is widespread, book dealers' catalogs, supplied lists, and dealer visits are also important selection tools for o.p. items.
- The respondents report that use of specialist art book dealers has either stayed about the same or even increased over the past few years and that the reputation of a known and trusted dealer remains an important factor in selecting a vendor.
- Nearly 60% of our responding libraries are offering a licensed digital image collection that is primarily being used to support student research.

- About half of our institutions have an in-house digitization program often focusing on conversion of existing slide collections or special collections.
- Few institutions offer credit classes on specialized art and/or architecture resources but 81% of the academic libraries are offering in-class lectures for undergraduate and graduate students.
- In addition to lacking adequate instructional space, staff resources for preparing and offering instruction is often insufficient. We also learned that lack of commitment from teaching faculty for library instruction may be a barrier and that little formal evaluation of instruction is being conducted.

We also can perceive some important differences between the types-of-libraries:

- Electronic journals are more common in academic libraries than in art museums or art schools likely due to the aggregators who include a few art and architecture titles among their offerings.
- Exchange programs are still an important factor for acquisitions in art museums although most institutions report a decline in receipts. It is also interesting that the majority of institutions who participate in an exchange program report the reason is to acquire material that otherwise might be unknown or not purchased.
- While nearly 70% of the academic libraries are offering electronic reserves, only 20% of the art and design libraries now provide that service.
- Although each type of library ranked traditional books, traditional journals, and the Internet as the 3 most popular formats for information, significant differences mark the next format choices. In academic libraries, e-journals, video, and CD-ROMs outranked microforms and e-books. In art museums, CD-ROMs and microforms are preferred over video, e-books, or e-journals. Art school libraries rated videos nearly as important as the top three formats but rated e-journals, CD-ROMs, microform, and e-books lower. This topic will be particularly interesting to track over the next few years.

The open comment section of the survey included many important points made by the respondents. Some unifying themes are inadequate space, challenges of adding new formats while maintaining traditional ones, staffing decreases, and the increasing demand for digital images. These issues may not be unique to art and architecture libraries but the survey now provides some documentation of how wide-spread the problems are.

It is my hope that this survey will be useful to institutions who need a measuring stick for their own art and architecture libraries as well as serve as a guide to some of our current practices in 2001-02. I further hope that a similar survey will be conducted periodically over the next few years so we can see how services and collections evolve in our libraries. For all of us who believe subject-specific libraries, such as art and architecture libraries, contribute value to our institutions, it is important that we do continual examination of our practices and procedures in order to justify our costs to administrators and to evaluate the quality of services provided to our patrons.

APPENDIX. Survey Results

	ACADEMIC	MUSEUM	SCHOOL	TOTAL
I. ENVIRONMENT *Circle only one answer for questions 1 & 2*				
1. Does your institution have a separate art or architecture library?				
a. yes	72	46	9	127
b. no	24	0	11	35
No Answer	1	0	0	1
2. Indicate the number of art & architecture volumes in your collection.				
a. 0-20,000 vols.	7	1	2	10
b. 20,000-50,000 vols.	14	16	12	42
c. 50,000-100,000 volumes	38	13	5	56
d. 100,000-200,000 volumes	25	9	1	35
e. 200,000-500,000 volumes	7	6	0	13
f. over 500,000 volumes	1	1	0	2
No Answer	5	0	0	5
II. FACILITIES *Circle only one answer for questions 1-3*				
1. For how long do you estimate that your current library will have sufficient space?				
a. 0-5 years	71	36	18	125
b. 6-10 years	14	6	1	21
c. 11-15 years	4	3	1	8
d. more than 16 years	6	1	0	7
No Answer	2	0	0	2

	ACADEMIC	MUSEUM	SCHOOL	TOTAL
2. If you answered "a" (0-5 years) to question II.1, what area of your facility is <u>most</u> deficient?				
a. collection space	69	36	11	116
b. staff space	1(2)	0(2)	2(1)	3(5)
c. reader space	0(1)	0(2)	2(1)	2(4)
d. instruction space	2(7)	0(2)	2	4(9)
e. equipment space	0(2)	1(2)	0(2)	1(6)
f. other?_____	5*	1	3*	9
No Answer	19	8	1	28

*all
() In this and subsequent questions where only one response was requested and when more than one answer was marked, one mark was counted and any additional marks are included in ().

3. If you answered "a" (0-5 years) to question II.1, what <u>primary</u> option do you think is most likely to be utilized to address the problem?				
a. building addition	5	2(1)	0	7(1)
b. moveable shelving	7(1)	7	2(1)	16(2)
c. off-site storage	44(4)	7(1)	3(2)	54(7)
d. use adjacent space	5(1)	7(2)**	4(2)	16(5)
e. library will move	9(2)	12	6	27(2)
f. other? _____	4*	1**	4***	9
No Answer	22	10	1	33

*renovation, weed, reorganize space, add shelving, move to the Main Library; **building renovation; ***reallocate space; weed; not-addressed; e-books

4. Which of these services & equipment does your library <u>currently</u> offer to your users?				
a. reference				
1. e-mail	91	40	11	142
2. phone	90	39	16	145
3. by appointment	89	32	15	136
4. staffed ref. desk	73	35	20	128
No Answer	1	1	0	2
b. instruction				
1. full credit class	11	0	3	14
2. in class lectures	81	9	16	106
3. workshops	57	13	10	80
4. tours	85	37	18	140
No Answer	2	8	0	10
c. workstations with				
1. Internet access	95	40	20	155
2. e-mail access only	31	4	4	39
3. licensed databases	93	36	19	148
4. word-processing	25	18*	12	55
5. database management	20	8	3	31
No Answer	1	4	0	5

*sometimes restricted to museum staff

APPENDIX (continued)

	ACADEMIC	MUSEUM	SCHOOL	TOTAL
d. photocopiers				
1. color	36	8	8	52
2. with book cradle	21	17	3	41
3. enlarging & reducing	85	44	20	149
No Answer	1	0	0	1
e. visual resources				
1. slide collection	28	24	19	71
2. videos	67	27	19	113
3. images on CD-ROMs	56	24	10	90
4. Images on microforms	53	17	6	76
No Answer	13	5	1	19
f. microform				
1. reader	53	15	6	74
2. reader-printer	48	32	9	89
No Answer	22	9	7	38
g. other equipment or services				
1. scanner station	39	12	12	63
2. light-tables	23	18	17	58
3. lockers	24	7	1	32
4. assigned seats	37	11	2	50
5. light-stand	39	14	12	65
6. other? _____	17*	2**	5***	24
No Answer	18	15	0	33

*color printing & plotting facility, opaque projector, slide projector, slide viewer, portable fiche reader, VCR, laptops, study rooms, printers, computer lab, ADA Zoom text, cameras, card-cash machine; lok mobile; Kurzweil machine; digital projector; analog to digital for audio, visual & video; **reserves, copier; ***media equipment; video monitors; VCR; slide projectors; DVD

III. ACQUISITIONS   *Circle only one answer for questions 1-7*

1. How are most of your <u>new</u> mainstream (university press & major publishers) books acquired?				
a. approval plan	71	9	7	87
b. publisher standing order	0(1)	0(1)	1	1(2)
c. individual firm order	21(7)	31(2)	12(1)	64(10)
d. other? _____	4*	6**	0	10
No Answer	1	0	0	1

*all; **gifts, museum bookstore

2. How are most of your exhibition catalogs and small press publications acquired?				
a. approval plan	55	5	8	68
b. publisher standing order	0(1)	1(1)	0	1(2)
c. on exchange	0(1)	22(3)	2	24(4)

	ACADEMIC	MUSEUM	SCHOOL	TOTAL
d. individual firm order	37(6)	15(4)	10	62(10)
e. other? _____	2*	3**	0	5
No Answer	3	0	0	3
*all, local bookstores; **gifts				
3. Does your library offer licensed art or architecture e-books?				
a. yes	49*	0	3	52
b. no	45	46	16	107
No Answer	3	0	1	4
*many respondents mention netLibrary or few e-books				
4. Does your library offer licensed art or architecture e-journals?				
a. yes	74	10	8	92
b. no	20	36	12	68
No Answer	3	0	0	3
5. Do you participate in an exchange program for exhibition catalogs?				
a. yes	20	44	8	72
b. no	75	2	12	89
No Answer	2	0	0	2
6. If you answered "a" (yes) to question III.5, are the number of exchange receipts				
a. increasing	1	6	1	8
b. decreasing	8	24	4	36
c. staying about the same	10	14	3	27
No Answer	78	2	12	92
7. If you answered "a" (yes) to question III.5, would you agree that the <u>primary</u> purpose of an exchange is				
a. in lieu of purchase	5	11(2)	1	17(2)
b. adds value to collection	14(1)	21(3)	5	40(4)
c. to place your institution's publications	1(3)	7(5)	1	9(8)
No Answer	79	5	14	98

8. Rank the following information formats for the most popular among the majority of your users for research and teaching. *Mark with numbers 1-8 (1 = most popular, 8 = least popular)*

ACADEMIC LIBRARIES

RANKED	1	2	3	4	5	6	7	8
Traditional book	82	6	5	2	0	0	0	0
Traditional journal	8	64	14	9	1	1	1	0
Internet	4	11	39	24	8	2	2	1
Electronic journal	5	8	23	22	15	5	8	0

APPENDIX (continued)

ACADEMIC LIBRARIES

RANKED	1	2	3	4	5	6	7	8
Video	0	0	6	18	23	15	9	6
CD-ROM	0	1	3	7	19	23	25	5
Microform	0	0	3	2	11	21	16	29
Electronic book	0	0	1	4	5	12	17	39

MUSEUM LIBRARIES

RANKED	1	2	3	4	5	6	7	8
Traditional book	44	2	0	0	0	0	0	0
Traditional journal	3	36	4	1	0	0	0	0
Internet	0	3	21	7	8	1	0	0
CD-ROM	0	0	1	21	8	6	0	0
Microform	0	1	11	7	8	4	1	2
Video	0	1	0	0	7	11	3	5
Electronic journal	0	0	2	2	2	5	9	4
Electronic book	0	0	0	0	0	3	9	9

ART SCHOOL LIBRARIES

RANKED	1	2	3	4	5	6	7	8
Traditional book	19	0	0	0	0	0	0	1
Traditional journal	0	13	3	2	1	0	0	1
Internet	0	3	9	5	1	0	0	0
Video	0	2	7	6	2	1	2	0
Electronic journal	1	0	0	2	6	5	1	1
CD-ROM	0	1	0	1	8	4	4	0
Microform	0	1	0	0	0	5	2	8
Electronic book	0	0	0	0	1	1	5	5

TOTALS FROM RESPONDENTS								
RANKED	1	2	3	4	5	6	7	8
Traditional book	145	8	5	2	0	0	0	1
Traditional journal	11	113	21	12	2	1	1	1
Internet	4	17	69	36	17	3	2	1
Electronic journal	6	8	25	26	23	15	18	5
Video	0	3	13	24	32	27	14	11
CD-ROM	0	2	4	29	35	33	29	5
Microform	0	2	13	9	19	30	19	39
Electronic book	0	0	1	4	6	16	31	53

	ACADEMIC	MUSEUM	SCHOOL	TOTAL
9. How are your out-of-print items acquired? *Circle all that apply*				
a. list to book dealer(s)	47	17	1	65
b. found in catalogs	65	27	4	96
c. found on-line	88	45	19	152
d. other? _____	12*	8**	3***	23
No Answer	1	0	0	1

*dealer visit, dealer suggestion, gifts, acquisitions dept. selects vendor, new book vendor's o.p. service; **dealer visit, gifts, book fairs, librarians & curators shop at o.p. dealers while traveling on international business; ***o.p. bookshops, approval plan through single vendor, direct

10. Over the past 5 years, has your use of specialist art book dealers for out-of-print items				
a. increased	24	21	7	52
b. decreased	22	9	5	36
c. stayed about the same	42	17	8	67
No Answer	8	0	0	8

11. How important is it to you that you purchase out-of-print material from a known dealer?				
a. only use dealers whose reputation I trust	14	6	1	21
b. prefer trusted dealers if the price is comparable	46	21	8	75
c. decision based on price and condition only	30	19	10	59
No Answer	7	0	1	8

IV. Digital				
1. Does your library offer any licensed Internet digital image collection? *Circle only one answer*				
a. yes	65	18	12	95
b. no	29	28	8	65
No Answer	3	0	0	3

APPENDIX (continued)

	ACADEMIC	MUSEUM	SCHOOL	TOTAL
2. If you answered "a" (yes) to question 1, which image collections? *Circle all that apply*				
a. AMICO	30	14	6	50
b. Bridgeman Art Library	41	5	4	50
c. Saskia Digital Image Sets	12	1	7	20
d. AccuNet/AP Multimedia	26	0	1	27
e. Index of Christian Art	33	5	0	38
f. other?_____	2*	4**	1***	7
No Answer	28	28	8	64
*Univ. of Michigan image service, Ebsco; **I-on-Art, FLW Drawings, museum's collection; Artnet; ***Artfact				
3. What is the <u>primary</u> use of the Internet digital image collection(s)? *Circle only one answer*				
a. teaching	11	4	7	22
b. student research	47(5)	4(1)	4(2)	55(8)
c. faculty or curatorial research	3(5)	13(1)	3	19(6)
d. other? _____	7	4	0	11
No Answer	27	23	6	58
4. Does your library have a digitization program for its collection? *Circle only one answer*				
a. yes	49	19	7	75
b. no	41	26	11	78
No Answer	7	1	2	10

5. If you answered yes to question IV.4, please describe the scope & purpose of the program including whether materials from the art or architecture collection are being digitized.

ACADEMIC LIBRARIES

Archives and special collection materials (not necessarily art); Library-wide effort but no art/arch participation yet; Art materials in special collections; Digitizing slide collection on demand; Digitize for reserves; Participate in the James Madison Univ. Digital Image Database project; Library-wide effort to digitization with some art books included; Grant related initiatives without an art/architecture focus; Slide collection; Posters, including an International Poster Collection from Special Collections; Periodicals; Photographs, including wildlife photos for the science curriculum; Postcards, including a specific project on Delaware postcards; Tsunami project; If o.p. title unavailable for purchase, it is borrowed, scanned, printed and bound; scanned files retained for a future project; Scanning for document delivery from photograph collection; Digital Library for Decorative Arts and Material Culture project; Artists' Book Collection project being planned; Amico contributor

MUSEUM LIBRARIES

Special portions of the collections (individual artists); Thumbnails for our collection database; Archival collections/grant funded; Rare books and manuscripts; Library special collections–documentary photographs and archives; Museum objects in the permanent collection; Adding images to online records for the slide collection; Future participation in RLG Cultural Materials Alliance; One to two titles are selected to digitize based on rarity, usefulness to research community, fragility, and quality of illustrations; Archival and special collections; Bulletins; Digitizing images from VR collection first plus requested images from Rare Book Room (if out of copyright); Intended to expand remote access to collections and reduce handling of fragile items; Preservation of rare materials; Make digitized images available for remote users; Works of art in our photo archive and other archival materials; Museum contributions to AMICO and museum website; Digitization of primary documents to (1) provide access; (2) allow for new research; (3) to preserve; Scanning of photography of museum's objects being done comprehensively; Architecture and Design Collection (Mellon funded); On-demand by Imaging Services Dept.; Greek vases for annual assignment (preservation and eventually, access remotely); Digitizing slides documenting early exhibitioons in the museum; Early audio tapes (artists' conversations) are being converted to digital CDs

ART SCHOOL LIBRARIES

Slide Library has recently begun a pilot project to digitize slides for one art history class, eventually will expand to support the entire curriculum; The entire collection will be digitized so that we can participate in AMICO's exchange; Scanning slides into digital format for projection and electronic reserves; Poster collections (difficult to handle in paper format so digitized version increased access); Photograph collection, esp. historical images; Digital Archive Online, a password protected image database to assist in teaching history of graphic design; Digitization of the slide collection; Digitizing slides not print materials for teaching and study purposes only; As needed by faculty

	ACADEMIC	MUSEUM	SCHOOL	TOTAL
6. Does your library offer electronic reserves? *Circle only one answer*				
a. yes	67	2	4	73
b. no	29	41	16	86
No Answer	1	3	0	4
V. Instruction *Circle only one answer for questions 1-4*				
1. Does your institution offer a credit class on library skills?				
a. yes	21	0	2	23
b. no	75	46	18	139
No Answer	1	0	0	1
2. Does your institution offer a credit class on specialized art and/or architecture resources?				
a. yes	7	1	0	8
b. no	89	45	20	154
No Answer	1	0	0	1
3. Does an art or architecture library staff member offer in-class lectures for other teachers?				
a. yes	79	15	16	110
b. no	14	31	4	49
No Answer	4	0	0	4
4. If you answered "a" (yes) to question V.3, do you believe the demand for such lectures is				
a. increasing	27	8	10	45
b. decreasing	8	1	2	11
c. staying about the same	45	5	4	54
No Answer	17	32	4	53
5. Does your library staff prepare individual handouts or web pages listing resources for specific classes?				
a. always	33	4	3	40
b. frequently	46	6	11	63
c. rarely	15	14	2	31
d. never	2	20	4	26
No Answer	1	2	0	3
6. Who is the audience for your library instruction? *Circle all that apply*				
a. general public	5	11	0	16

APPENDIX (continued)

	ACADEMIC	MUSEUM	SCHOOL	TOTAL
b. K-12 students	2	3	0	5
c. undergraduate students	87	17	19	123
d. graduate students	85	27	14	126
e. faculty and/or curators	42	35	5	82
f. museum docents	16	33	1	50
No Answer	1	2	0	3
7. Do you offer a program for guided, self-paced library instruction? *Circle only one answer*				
a. yes	37	2	6	45
b. no	59	44	14	117
No Answer	1	0	0	1
8. If you answered "a" (yes) to question V.7, do you use *Circle all that apply*				
a. printed path-finders	11	3	3	17
b. web pages	32	0	2	34
c. interactive computer programs	10	0	2	12
d. other? _____	0	0	1*	1
No Answer	59	43	14	116
*personal tutorials				
9. What are the barriers to an increased instruction program in your library? *Circle all that apply*				
a. space	45	7	9	61
b. preparation time	41	18	5	64
c. administrative support	10	10	7	27
d. user interest	40	18	14	72
e. appropriate equipment	27	4	10	41
f. other? _____	26*	14**	5***	45
No Answer	3	2	0	5
*staff shortage, faculty support, money, departmental support, teaching skills of librarians; **staff shortage, restricted access, mission, none, time to provide actual instruction; ***faculty commitment, no dedicated computer lab, needs outreach, none				
10. How is your instruction effort evaluated? *Circle all that apply*				
a. formal evaluations	28	5	5	38
b. informal feedback	75	20	10	105
c. peer reviewed	10	2	3	15
d. no evaluation	20	22	6	48
e. other? _____	5*	0	1**	6
No Answer	2	5	0	7
*pre-test/post-test; questionnaire; statistics; instruction librarian review; random solicited feedback, usually by email; **biennial library survey				
Is there anything else about your efforts to provide library space, integrate digital image collections into the library, offer library instruction, or about the impact of e-commerce on library acquisitions that you'd like to tell me?				

ACADEMIC LIBRARIES

FUNDING

Inadequate funding affects all areas of operations so a variety of measures are constantly unfurled

SPACE

Groundbreaking in 2004; Running parallel libraries, analog and digital, with space and monetary needs for both; Moving older items to storage means the historic nature of the collection is less coherent; Need to add shelving capacity and implement selection of offsite storage; Most complex space issues are for storage of atypical formats such as architectural drawings, framed art, double folios; May need to review storeroom and office space for shelving; Space is good, 14,000 sq. ft. opened in 1997; Out of space so books that haven't circulated for 10 years going to storage; New combined art/architecture library planned for 2007; A&A Library likely to be reincorporated into the Main Library within the next 5 years; About to break ground for a huge, state-of-the-art depository; Moving into a renovated facility that is too small for the collection so will be storing the equivalent of 10-years growth off-site; Have about 10,000 volumes in a remote area and will send more every year; Use of offsite storage of 30,000 volumes was intended to be interim but more likely will be long-term—even with 24 hr. turn-around, it changes the way collections are used; In the design phase for a new facility that will increase space from 5700 sq. ft to 9000 sq. ft.

COLLECTIONS

Subscriptions to new journals inadequate for program support; Growth of electronic resources mostly positive but comes at the expense of the print collection; Investment in e-databases must be supported by equipment to view, manipulate and print the data retrieved; Consortial buying is important for expensive resources; Web resources enable work with remote vendors; Dichotomy between the library and the v.r. collection is an issue, who should buy large sets?

INSTRUCTION

Philosophically prefers interpersonal reference over instruction; Need instructional space within the library; Need to provide bookable seminar room/group study space with connectivity; Revamping library web pages and will add instruction and info pages; Slight decrease in demand for instruction likely due to use of library's subject guides on the Web; Demand for instruction is growing with 6-7 classes in January alone; Classes are large and space is inadequate; Use of a laptop for instruction when feasible but digital projector availability is limited; Hard to make content of instruction relevant since most of the traditional art reference sources aren't useful for interdisciplinary and popular culture topics; Good web pages facilitate research; Increasing web-based efforts for instruction and library literacy; One of the major challenges in our profession is in the amount of time devoted to in-class presentations of online databases, their contents, their use. Administration wants us to do this work, but faculty are only occasionally eager for us to use class time. We also need to be better trained in how to provide such instruction. All this takes time, which is always in short supply. We also need time to evaluate non-licensed Web sites for our users, who often assume that information on the Net is the *only* information they need, without worrying about its validity; In regard to the Internet as a source of information, I think student expectations and experience upon entering college is growing faster than faculty and institutional knowledge and support.

IN-PERSON USE OF THE LIBRARY

Circulation stats have decreased; Need to promote the library as good communal/intellectual space; Using live digital reference using LSSI software; Now assessing the proper mix of reference services, real person at desk, email, digital reference, to see how we can best serve our users; A pilot program with "chat" reference.

DIGITIZATION

Effort not yet 1-yr old at this institution; Use of digital image collection so far is rather low; Image collection growing both through faculty requests for slides and budget-supported acquisition of digital images; The demand for digitized color images and the lack of a color printer, copier, or photo-stand in the library has created pressure to circulate unbound journals; Copyright problems viewed as library problems by faculty who want to add digitized images to their web pages and show them in classes; Amico is too expensive; Hope that ArtStor will be available eventually; Digital image reserves available for 3 years and demand has risen dramatically; University has purchased The Gallery System software and will create a digital image database that will be accessed over the web; Images are less important than text (to the administrators); Issue between library and v.r. collection as to what front end should be used.

APPENDIX (continued)

E-COMMERCE

Increased number of vendors; Increased use of credit card transactions and reduced flow of invoices; E-commerce has made acquisition of o.p. materials much easier.

LIBRARY SECURITY

Online catalogs combined with e-commerce makes it easy for thieves to identify valuable materials in specific collections; Razored plates hard to detect and protect; How to protect "medium rare" collections.

COMMUNICATIONS

Distributes a "newsletter" to the Art faculty each Fall and Spring offering classes and information on new electronic products.

STAFFING

Interim art librarian who still has her/his "regular" position and the loss of the staff assistant position; Budgets and staff are shrinking so we need to do more with less; Lost 30% of the staff positions in the A&A Library since 1990; Always more to do than there are people to do it; Increasing demands for electronic services without commensurate increases in staff support.

MUSEUM LIBRARIES

INSTRUCTION

The conservator and I present a connoisseurship block (12-16 hours) on the printed book as part of the museum's graduate program curriculum for credit; We hope to offer more whole-class orientation tours or a PowerPoint presentation in classrooms in the near future; We make visits to curators in their offices to teach them how to access our subscription databases that relate to their subject areas; Our library instruction is one-on-one, specific to the reader's field, background, and project(s); We do offer self-guided brochure for researching artists by name and for researching information on museum's objects.

SPACE

Our space was recently reduced by half when library space was converted to curatorial offices and storage; Library space will double with museum expansion in 2006; Our answer to facilities would have been 0-5 years had we not recently undertaken considerable projects to weed collections, sell extraneous and duplicate materials, consolidate shelves, shift stacks. This gave us breathing room for another few years while we evaluate compact shelving, building expansion, and/or off-site storage.

DIGITIZATION

All efforts to find funding to digitize rare materials have failed; Digital images exist in a completely separate department so it would be a hugely political act to combine the library and the imaging departments; As a museum library, we have access to our permanent collection online.

ADMINISTRATION

We are part of a campus library system and therefore have access to specialized sources but our holdings are becoming increasingly specialized; Impediments come from the administration making staffing decisions without knowledge of a library's operation; Too little $$, too little staff; Our library is small; I am the only staff person so most of your survey does not apply to our library; All come back to budget, staff time and space. The more we get of any of above, the more we tend to provide; Finding support staff is increasingly difficult.

COLLECTIONS

Our visual resources include a photo study collection of 2 million images; I prefer dealing with vendors I know and trust but find that not to be practical in most instances.

ART SCHOOL LIBRARIES

E-COMMERCE

E-notices from publishers alerting me to new publications can be useful; We make credit card purchases on Amazon.com; We have successfully used E-Bay to sell unwanted gifts.

DIGITAL

We are actively planning to switch from slides to digital images for use in teaching within 5 years; We're waiting for better collections to come out.

COLLECTIONS

One of the major problems is that the options for electronic resources, i.e., licensed databases, digital collections, have skyrocketed while our acquisitions budget remains the same; There is still a high demand for traditional books and our funds cannot stretch to meet all formats.

Index

Pages followed by *t* indicate tables; those followed by *f* indicate figures; and those followed by *n* indicate notes.

http://www.haworthpress.com/store/product.asp?sku=J111
© 2003 by The Haworth Press, Inc. All rights reserved.
10.1300/J111v39n01_07

Access, Ownership, and Resource Sharing, edited by Sul H. Lee (Vol. 20, No. 1, 1995). *The contributing authors present a useful and informative look at the current status of information provision and some of the challenges the subject presents.*

Libraries as User-Centered Organizations: Imperatives for Organizational Change, edited by Meredith A. Butler (Vol. 19, No. 3/4, 1994). *"Presents a very timely and well-organized discussion of major trends and influences causing organizational changes." (Science Books & Films)*

Declining Acquisitions Budgets: Allocation, Collection Development and Impact Communication, edited by Sul H. Lee (Vol. 19, No. 2, 1994). *"Expert and provocative. . . . Presents many ways of looking at library budget deterioration and responses to it . . . There is much food for thought here." (Library Resources & Technical Services)*

The Role and Future of Special Collections in Research Libraries: British and American Perspectives, edited by Sul H. Lee (Vol. 19, No. 1, 1993). *"A provocative but informative read for library users, academic administrators, and private sponsors." (International Journal of Information and Library Research)*

Catalysts for Change: Managing Libraries in the 1990s, edited by Gisela M. von Dran, DPA, MLS, and Jennifer Cargill, MSLS, MSed (Vol. 18, No. 3/4, 1994). *"A useful collection of articles which focuses on the need for librarians to employ enlightened management practices in order to adapt to and thrive in the rapidly changing information environment." (Australian Library Review)*

Integrating Total Quality Management in a Library Setting, edited by Susan Jurow, MLS, and Susan B. Barnard, MLS (Vol. 18, No. 1/2, 1993). *"Especially valuable are the librarian experiences that directly relate to real concerns about TQM. Recommended for all professional reading collections." (Library Journal)*

Leadership in Academic Libraries: Proceedings of the W. Porter Kellam Conference, The University of Georgia, May 7, 1991, edited by William Gray Potter (Vol. 17, No. 4, 1993). *"Will be of interest to those concerned with the history of American academic libraries." (Australian Library Review)*

Collection Assessment and Acquisitions Budgets, edited by Sul H. Lee (Vol. 17, No. 2, 1993). *Contains timely information about the assessment of academic library collections and the relationship of collection assessment to acquisition budgets.*

Developing Library Staff for the 21st Century, edited by Maureen Sullivan (Vol. 17, No. 1, 1992). *"I found myself enthralled with this highly readable publication. It is one of those rare compilations that manages to successfully integrate current general management operational thinking in the context of academic library management." (Bimonthly Review of Law Books)*

Vendor Evaluation and Acquisition Budgets, edited by Sul H. Lee (Vol. 16, No. 3, 1992). *"The title doesn't do justice to the true scope of this excellent collection of papers delivered at the sixth annual conference on library acquisitions sponsored by the University of Oklahoma Libraries." (Kent K. Hendrickson, BS, MALS, Dean of Libraries, University of Nebraska-Lincoln) Find insightful discussions on the impact of rising costs on library budgets and management in this groundbreaking book.*

The Management of Library and Information Studies Education, edited by Herman L. Totten, PhD, MLS (Vol. 16, No. 1/2, 1992). *"Offers something of interest to everyone connected with LIS education–the undergraduate contemplating a master's degree, the doctoral student struggling with courses and career choices, the new faculty member aghast at conflicting responsibilities, the experienced but stressed LIS professor, and directors of LIS Schools." (Education Libraries)*

Library Management in the Information Technology Environment: Issues, Policies, and Practice for Administrators, edited by Brice G. Hobrock, PhD, MLS (Vol. 15, No. 3/4, 1992). *"A road map to identify some of the alternative routes to the electronic library." (Stephen Rollins, Associate Dean for Library Services, General Library, University of New Mexico)*

Managing Technical Services in the 90's, edited by Drew Racine (Vol. 15, No. 1/2, 1991). *"Presents an eclectic overview of the challenges currently facing all library technical services efforts. . . . Recommended to library administrators and interested practitioners." (Library Journal)*

Budgets for Acquisitions: Strategies for Serials, Monographs, and Electronic Formats, edited by Sul H. Lee (Vol. 14, No. 3, 1991). *"Much more than a series of handy tips for the careful shopper. This [book] is a most useful one—well-informed, thought-provoking, and authoritative." (Australian Library Review)*

Creative Planning for Library Administration: Leadership for the Future, edited by Kent Hendrickson, MALS (Vol. 14, No. 2, 1991). *"Provides some essential information on the planning process, and the mix of opinions and methodologies, as well as examples relevant to every library manager, resulting in a very readable foray into a topic too long avoided by many of us." (Canadian Library Journal)*

Strategic Planning in Higher Education: Implementing New Roles for the Academic Library, edited by James F. Williams, II, MLS (Vol. 13, No. 3/4, 1991). *"A welcome addition to the sparse literature on strategic planning in university libraries. Academic librarians considering strategic planning for their libraries will learn a great deal from this work." (Canadian Library Journal)*

Personnel Administration in an Automated Environment, edited by Philip E. Leinbach, MLS (Vol. 13, No. 1/2, 1990). *"An interesting and worthwhile volume, recommended to university library administrators and to others interested in thought-provoking discussion of the personnel implications of automation." (Canadian Library Journal)*

Library Development: A Future Imperative, edited by Dwight F. Burlingame, PhD (Vol. 12, No. 4, 1990). *"This volume provides an excellent overview of fundraising with special application to libraries. . . . A useful book that is highly recommended for all libraries." (Library Journal)*

Library Material Costs and Access to Information, edited by Sul H. Lee (Vol. 12, No. 3, 1991). *"A cohesive treatment of the issue. Although the book's contributors possess a research library perspective, the data and the ideas presented are of interest and benefit to the entire profession, especially academic librarians." (Library Resources and Technical Services)*

Training Issues and Strategies in Libraries, edited by Paul M. Gherman, MALS, and Frances O. Painter, MLS, MBA (Vol. 12, No. 2, 1990). *"There are . . . useful chapters, all by different authors, each with a preliminary summary of the content—a device that saves much time in deciding whether to read the whole chapter or merely skim through it. Many of the chapters are essentially practical without too much emphasis on theory. This book is a good investment." (Library Association Record)*

Library Education and Employer Expectations, edited by E. Dale Cluff, PhD, MLS (Vol. 11, No. 3/4, 1990). *"Useful to library-school students and faculty interested in employment problems and employer perspectives. Librarians concerned with recruitment practices will also be interested." (Information Technology and Libraries)*

Managing Public Libraries in the 21st Century, edited by Pat Woodrum, MLS (Vol. 11, No. 1/2, 1989). *"A broad-based collection of topics that explores the management problems and possibilities public libraries will be facing in the 21st century." (Robert Swisher, PhD, Director, School of Library and Information Studies, University of Oklahoma)*

Human Resources Management in Libraries, edited by Gisela M. Webb, MLS, MPA (Vol. 10, No. 4, 1989). *"Thought provoking and enjoyable reading. . . . Provides valuable insights for the effective information manager." (Special Libraries)*

Creativity, Innovation, and Entrepreneurship in Libraries, edited by Donald E. Riggs, EdD, MLS (Vol. 10, No. 2/3, 1989). *"The volume is well worth reading as a whole. . . . There is very little repetition, and it should stimulate thought." (Australian Library Review)*

The Impact of Rising Costs of Serials and Monographs on Library Services and Programs, edited by Sul H. Lee (Vol. 10, No. 1, 1989). *". . . Sul Lee hit a winner here." (Serials Review)*